WAY
FORWARD
FOR AFRICA

WAY FORWARD FOR AFRICA

GEORGE NGWANE

MAP

Kansas City, MO

Way Forward For Africa
by George Ngwane

First published 2013

Miraclaire Academic Publications (MAP)
8400 East 92nd Terrace, Kansas City, MO 64138, USA

ISBN (10): 0-6157-4690-X / ISBN (13): 978-0-6157-4690-6

Printed in the United States of America

MAP is an imprint of Miraclaire Publishing LLC
www.miraclairepublishing.com

Foreword

Africa is a continent replete with amazing contradictions; it is generally acclaimed to be the cradle of civilization, it possesses huge and mouth whetting human and natural resources. In fact, it is a continent blessed with nature's prodigality. Yet, it is also a continent that harbours a third of the world's poorest countries and a population which has been emasculated socially, politically and economically.

African scholars as well as their Africanist counterparts have been alive to the debate as to why the continent's fate has remained on the edge of a precipice. Through prismatic spectrums such scholars have appreciated Africa's problems from Afrocentric, Eurocentric, radical and conservative perspectives. The culmination of their collective efforts is an avalanche of literatures on Africa.

Useful as these contributions are, most of them have remained at the conceptual / theoretical and intellectual levels, offering very little practical solutions to the continent's ever-increasing problems. George Ngwane's *Way Forward for Africa* is a refreshing departure from the stereotype. It is a compendious and kaleidoscopic appreciation of the continent's problems, suggesting the way forward. Shorn of any rhetorical obfuscation and verbiage, the study, in ninety eight pages, four chapters, and in scintillating language diagnoses and prescribes practical solutions to the woes of the continent.

i

The first chapter, which centres on the African youths, is an insightful categorization of the youths into three groups: the complacent, wasted and critical generations. The first two categories have been caught up in a web of docility and are inextricably entangled in a morass of dialectical materialism. They see themselves as a generation under perpetual siege and, accordingly, have to dance to the dictates of the moment. They hold no promise for Africa. The critical generation, perhaps, holds the magic wand; it is charged with charting the continent through the contours of its development efforts. The crucial role of youths in the development process of any given society is not a matter opened to debate: no country ever thrives without the active participation of its youths in this process.

Chapter two, like chapter three, centres on democracy with a razor thin distinction between them. The former argues that Africa's pristine governing institutions had all the trappings of modern democratic practices. Unfortunately, however, with the intrusion of colonialism there was a wholesale imposition of Western democratic values which were not only incongruent with the African reality but which were tailored to meet Western designs.

Against this grim background, the latter chapter, the penultimate, surveys the various democratic options opened to Africa in what Ngwane styles "Innovative choices": umbrella democracy, no party democracy, consociational democracy and monarchical democracy. The author's critique of the "Conservative Choice" i.e. multiparty democracy under such rubrics as "multiparty politics and state paralysis and multiparty democracy and state authority" is most instructive and paradigmatic of the political quagmire in which Cameroon has been submerged.

Chapter four, the last, attempts to align individually country-based development efforts in the continent with a holistic, continent-oriented strategy under the aegis of the African Union. Ngwane, a consummate Pan-Africanist, proposes two alternatives: a five –tiered federation of African regions based on the existing North, South, West, East and Central regions to replace the fifty-three countries in the continent; and an African Union akin to the European Union (EU).

The author has remarkably made a long and tortuous story short and simple without smothering complexities. His grasp of the travails of the continent is impressive, so is his objectivity and even handedness. His literary style is crisp and a sheer delight. His study is not intended to portray Africa as in a state of dystopia as most works do. A huge continent with a prickly and dynamic population, Africa enjoys tantalizingly bright potentials. She could compare with other advanced continents of the world if its economy as well as other socio-political variables are repositioned and refocused on their proper growth paths. With a potentially huge market, the labour absorptive capacity of its economy can be vastly energized and made more resilient than at present. This is what Ngwane's *Way Forward for Africa* advocates. This book should be amongst the prized collections of any library worth its salt on African issues.

Canute A. Ngwa, Ph.D,

CONTENTS

CHAPTER ONE
AFRICAN YOUTH MUST ARISE

African Youth can be classified into three generations:
(i)   the complacent generation,
(ii)   the wasted generation
(iii)   the critical generation.

Complacent Generation

The complacent generation comprises youth who see ills in their society and are fully aware of the dire consequences such ills can have but prefer to turn a blind eye and deaf ear to them. Motivated by the urge to survive, the youths become appendages of the mainstream decadent status quo. They are disillusioned with the system but feel they can make some economic gains from its predatory politics before it finally collapses.   Triggered by the gluttonous metaphor that "if you can't beat them, join them", they have been emasculated by the mystery of incumbency. Apart from their cravings to live parasitically on the system, their alliance is founded on a mutual agreement of self-protection. The system protects them through advancements in their administrative careers, encourages them in state robbery and provides them with immunity in their white collar thievery.   In return, the youths serve as doormats for the system's authoritarian boots and are prepared to sing songs concordant with the system's tune. This generation regards politics as a pure business enterprise in which the state is taken ransom for pecuniary benefits. The state is a prey; a forest that will continuously expand even if the persistent and indiscriminate depletion of its resources is a signal of extinction. However, what is peculiar with this class is that though greed is their motivating element, it is equipped with the faculty to prophesise when the feast will be over.

This generation possesses a rare and dangerous intellect to go with the wind and fit squarely in the pattern of any changing order. In other words, it possesses a wealth of logic that justifies its existence as amphibians adapting on political land and water. Educated? Yes! But as a means of seeking prominence and fulfilling its self-interest. Any intellectual argument based on good governance or self-reliance is regarded as mere sterile debate void of stirring any meaningful change. In its nauseating obsession with the status quo, this class has become hostile to any innovations. It discounts new and fertile ideas as figments of imagination of idealists and detractors. It regards itself realists who have judiciously weighed the gains of conservatism and the prospects of change and have come to the conclusion that "it is better to live with the devil you know than with the angel you don't know."

This complacent generation should not be mistaken for being dull and ignorant. On the contrary some of the finest scholars in the continent have been the spokespersons of this current of thought. These youths may be cowards and hypocrites saying in public what they do not believe in private but they are certainly not dull.

They may be opportunists seeking every avenue to join the ruling cartel of exploiters and oppressors, but they are not ignorant. They constitute dynamites that threaten the stability, progress and development of Africa. Their heart-mines are more hazardous than landmines. Indeed, it is this class that manufactures the obnoxious politics of an anti-people establishment. It wields so much power that it cannot be ignored. Either as individuals or voluntary aggregates, it makes its voice heard and impact so felt that lie-telling and vain promising have become an art.

One of the achievements of any democratic system is to produce a strong civil society. A strong civil society presupposes the creation of voluntary organisations, lobby groups and non-governmental organisations that enhance the welfare of the community. Once again, this class has proliferated the society with lobby groups that fan the flames of government mediocrity. It has failed to capture the charisma of earlier groups in Africa which used solidarity, traditional associations and youth leagues to articulate the interest of the masses. Instead, this generation knows its interest lies in its survival but hypocritically hoodwinks the gullible masses into believing that it is working for their interest.

It is therefore evident that the complacent generation of Africans does not believe in nation building, let alone African renaissance. Africa, to these youths, is for sale to the highest and mightiest Western bidder. What matters to them is how they can share national spoils born out of provoked ethnic animosities. Through their parochial lenses, they cry wolf when their interest is at stake and galvanize the sentiments of the masses against those they label "apostles of disunity and disintegration". They now mount on the dais of power to lambaste the so-called "sources of discord". But we know, as well as they do, that if the pillars of national unity are in flames today they struck the first match. It is this first match that has torched the very foundation of national cohesion and African solidarity. The vision of this class is antithetical to that of Pan-Africanists who saw Africa as a collective whole. Faced with state deficiencies, this class prefers to take shelter in empty ethnic shells, not to sing the redemptive songs of a national consensus but to propagate the confrontational dirges of a national suicide. It treats Africa as a conquered continent that must adopt or adapt to Western values. African unity is a quixotic adventure to be left in the realms of sloganeering. Yes, this class has cynically watched Africa descend to the chasm of disintegration, neo-colonial cleavages and marginalisation. With this generation virtually enjoying the political limelight of their countries, Africa has no way forward.

3

Since the leadership of Africa is saddled with or linked to such a class, progress is bound to stagnate on the same spot. The continent will continue to grow stale as long as it listens to the bankrupt ideas of this class. It is therefore probable that Africa may continue to be defined by this class through Western standards. For indeed, although it is more grounded in African culture and is "psychologically more protected from the ravages of colonially induced cultural self-denial, this class quietly accepts the superiority of Western culture and see immersion in this away from its roots as a means of achieving social and economic elevation" (Prah, 1997: 17). It is therefore quick to point out democratic achievements in Africa just because the Western manifestation of democracy is conspicuous. It also points out how long it took the West to accomplish its own democratic feat, and that given time, Africa, too, will develop on Western models. The occasional and often meagre economic accomplishments made by African countries utilizing conditional international aid and loans cited as evidence that Africa is making progress.

The greatest peril in front of us lies in the fact that Africa will wallow in the mire of dependency and domination as long as this class plays a central role in our democratic and developmental process.

Wasted Generation

In contrast to the complacent generation discussed above, the wasted generation has completely given up on its country's systems and Africa's leadership; no political debate can rouse it from its escapist slumber. It is a class whose vision for Africa is steeped in defeatism or nonchalance. To be fair, some of these youths did attempt to contribute to nation building but due to the resistance to change, they retreated and became passive pedestrians on the political highway. They have come to the perturbing conclusion that nothing workable can come out of this continent.

This class has been caught in the vicious web of Christianity, colonisation, and civilisation. Among other things the "White man of God" succeeded in eradicating the cultural values of the African by persuading him to see salvation not from his ancestral link but from a mythology whose origins could not be tied to local religious background. Even though African tribes told stories of their own mythology and some even went ahead to build their own shrines of worship, early missionaries used contempt and arrogance to deny the existence of an African Pantheon. Christianity was simply a form of worship dictated by the literature of the white missionaries, an onslaught on the political and cultural solidarity of the African collective psyche. It all seemed like groundwork prepared to facilitate manipulation and domination by eventual colonial governance. Its litany verses of meekness, humility, obedience and unalloyed subservience to God took hold of the African that until today most Africans allow the fate of their continent to be decided by the omniscience of God. While the Whiteman continues to build industries to accelerate development, the African takes pride in building churches to receive salvation. While the Whiteman invents what God has created, the African imitates what the Whiteman has invented. While the Whiteman draws inspiration from the adage that "God helps those who help themselves" the African still recites the biblical adage that "God's time is the best." While the Whiteman believes that a better society can only be forged from hard work, the African sees his prosperity only through prayers. This magic of hard work that under girds Western development and the opium of religion that consumes developmental energy in Africa, accounts, to some extent, for the developmental gap between Africa and Western nations.

All that is left for the wasted generation is to look at Europe with awe and bury its developmental potential in the incantation of prayer.

Having immersed itself in self-denial and self-psychosis, this generation is in a wild crusade to live according to the dictates of alien values. After the seeds of meekness and humility found fertile ground in African minds and hearts, the logical outcome was for colonialists to foist a government of repression in our traditional political system. The effects of the traumatic rape and concubinage of our political system will be addressed in a latter chapter. For now, it should suffice to say that despite decades of evolution, this class of Africans continues to hold with unprecedented aura, the supremacy of Europe and America over Africa. It is convinced that the destiny of Africa cannot be extricated from its dependency on the West. No doubt, nostalgia of colonial rule still recur today and African countries still map out themselves into colonial cleavages like Francophonie, Commonwealth, Lusophonie and bickering ensues from these colonial linguistic tags. The Anjouan Island in Comoros insisted on seceding because it wanted to go back to French rule. Some members of the wasted generation, like baby kangaroos running back to their mother's pouch, still want colonial masters to come back and directly rule.

Lulled by the fanaticism of religion, entangled in the bondage of colonialism, this class is dazzled by the mirage of Western civilisation. It imitates taste without borrowing Western skills. It has acquired a consumption pattern that is incompatible with its productive capacity. And so, vital energies of creativity have been wasted in ludicrous copy-catting. Latent talent has been sacrificed on the altar of cheap commercial graft. The class has become an assorted group of blind parrots - seeing nothing in its traditional past which it calls obsolete and primitive; seeing nothing in originality and self-reliance; denying the very

6

essence of the African personality. It has rejected all Africa stands for and is paradoxically going to where the West is escaping from. Its role models are not those who bring repute and prestige to developmental projects in Africa, but those who represent the myth created by cultural imperialism. Castrated by "Western cultural over-kill and invaded by the psychosis of self-hate, this class has dumped hyper Eurocentric garbage on our doorsteps with the aim of getting us to turn our backs on our origins. Yet we have seen a chain of Western philosophical vogues come and go without transforming or translating themselves into the betterment of the quality of life of African humanity" (Prah, 1997: 15). And so these young people see their dressing style, mannerisms, consumption pattern, and dreams of a better life through the Western spectacles - thanks to the ubiquitous images of the Western media. Having not bothered to know where it is from, this generation does not know where it is going. It is a kind of generation the Americans call "Generation X." The twin evils of cultural subjugation and untargeted educational system have produced a generation that is sunk neck-deep in the quagmire of mental slavery. Contented with second hand goods, it has cultivated a second hand mentality that destroys any effort towards autocentric development. Faced with any crisis (which in other countries is the mother of invention) these youths embark on another slave voyage to the West. Our great grandparents resisted slavery in 1492; some of them preferred to die en route than be transported across the Atlantic Ocean. They resisted this immoral and inhuman act that caused Africa both natural and human losses. If they were a given a chance, our great grandparents would have invested their labour in the land of our ancestors. Today, this breed of wasted generation offers to enslave itself to "God's own country," not because it wants to harvest the experiences of the West to build its own communities but because in the West, "money is quick to make." Once in the Diaspora, the youths start learning the social sciences of cultural adulteration and language affectation - their voices and views are acclimatised to the winter, summer and spring of discordant success. Ebini Atem, a committed Pan-Africanist living in America, had this observation to make of his roommate:

I have the opportunity of hosting in my apartment a young man from Sierra Leone, who had to leave the university residence. My young friend is a second year political science and pre-law student and we have great intellectual exchanges on issues relating to political and social Africa. The more I discussed with my young friend, the more I realised that most Africans still embark on the journey of academia for all the wrong reasons (1997: 9).

Ebini's narration presents a profile of a young man who leaves socio-political problems to melt in the sunshine of escapism - one whose mind is stuck to the religious tenet that "All is in God's hands," knowing pretty well that God's hands are already full with African problems, and that until Africans themselves start taking the plough in their own hands, God will never provide them with the energy to get going. Of course, there is nothing wrong with going West. The controversy lies in the purpose and outcome of this adventurous journey. The children of our great grandparents like W.E.B. Dubois and Marcus Garvey used their time in the Diaspora to organize Pan-African congresses. Some, such as Reverend Leon Sullivan used it to build bridges to Africa.

Why then do African youths escape to the West and forget about Africa? Why are the young so infatuated with the glamour of instant wealth that they cannot make material and human contribution to the welfare of Africa? In the confines of my solitude I sometimes sympathise with this generation for allowing the winds of despair and defeat to carry it to the shores of the Pacific Ocean. One of the reasons these young people have turned their backs on

Africa is that the bulk of African leaders has confiscated the future of these young people. Years after independence, most African leaders continue to pillage and plunder their own countries through cosmetic democratic reforms. The leaders continue to tell the young that they are leaders of tomorrow even though all is set for the dusk of leadership to eclipse the existence of these youths. The leadership of Africa has continued to deceive its own people and in some cases to incarcerate and eliminate those who have spoken against their ruling dynasties.

Critical Generation

In spite of this harassment and even death, there is a generation that has refused to be cowed, or dragooned into submission. I call this the critical generation because it believes that the future of any society is invested in its youths and youths are a reflection of its society and vice versa. This class therefore continues to raise its apocalyptic voice above the hullabaloo of the complacent and the wasted. It has not only persistently warned of a greater holocaust for Africa if the path of reason is abandoned, but has proposed credible alternatives for democracy and development that can usher this continent into its rightful historical position. The class is committed to social justice, home-grown economic development and consensual democracy. Ironically, this class is often snubbed, just regarded as a bunch of daydreamers, a group of alarmists who have lost all visions of political reality. This class is hardly given a chance to sing its constructive hymn. In its place, stooges and sycophants outsmart each other blaring their dismal vision for the continent. Yet this class continues to ask questions where others are silent and apathetic. It keeps asking why when others are asking why not. It is undaunted in its search for African unity, relentless in its effort to usher in a new wave of Pan-Africanism.

There have been three waves of Pan-Africanism. The first wave was what could be termed the anti-racist Pan-Africanism; it was concerned with the search for a common ancestry. It focused on African identity and assumed a cultural dimension. The second wave could be termed the anti-colonial Pan-Africanism because it was concerned with the search for a political freedom. It focused on independence and assumed a political dimension. The third wave of Pan-Africanism is what is being articulated by the critical generation. It can be termed African-nationalist Pan-Africanism because it focuses on an indigenous African statehood and assumes a multilateral dimension. Although African nationalism has existed under the banner of Pan-African movements "it was the product not of the Kleistian chauvinism but a mixture of anti-racism and which amounted, in practice to the same thing of anti-colonialism. Let freedom come and freedom will bring its own good solution" (Davidson, 1992: 165). Apart from isolated cases, neither freedom nor good solution has come to Africa. It is for this reason that the critical generation is bent on forging a new political, cultural and economic order for Africa.

This class has critically examined the fate of Africa and has come to the conclusion that the continent is at risk of a worse Sovietisation. In spite of all the verbalisation of a global village, Africa is still a victim of global pillage because globalisation has been perceived as the unification of cultural space. Africa, that began as a cultural entity and was perceived over the years as a viable political platform, is yielding to the tentacles of ethno-nationalism. What slavery and colonialism did to Africa was to despoil it of human resources and milk its natural resources. Today's Africa is a patched network of predatory states fighting to hold their egoistic own in a world where solidarity and unity have become buzzwords. More than a century ago, people of African descent held historic conferences to recapture the image and personality of the African and to reject stereotyped views that depicted a people who came from a thick dense forest of darkness. These visionaries lit the first candle of Pan Africanism to see the light of their common ancestry. They asserted themselves culturally and emboldened their identity as a people with a glorious past. It is indeed this search for a common ancestry that gave rise to the holistic perception of a continent defined not by colonial impositions of geographical boundaries, but through the Pan-African prism, that a single historical polity was seen. Arguably, the pioneer Pan-Africanists had a hazy notion of their past but the urge to mould a viable present and future gave an impetus to the second wave of Pan-Africanists who saw decolonisation as leverage to African unity. Unfortunately, because of the parochial interest of the pre-independence leadership, Africa lost the dream of Kwame Nkrumah that would have transformed this continent into one of co-ordinated opportunities and harmonised achievements. This may all be history now, but of what use is history if we cannot learn anything from it? History is the clock of human progress and the compass of development - it must be constantly consulted to make amends. Scholars have sometimes argued that the birth of the Organisation of African Unity (O.A.U) in Addis Ababa led to the death of genuine African unity. The unity of the O. A. U. had been cocooned in the interest of the leaders, not the people. Summits of the O.A. U. had sugar-coated the essence of African unity without rekindling the spirit of true Pan-Africanism. Of course concerted effort especially by the secretariat of the O. A. U. had been especially admirable but all attempts to translate this vision into concrete reality had been stalled by the lack of political will on the part of the lacklustre heads of member states. The result was that even the national boundaries that the heads of states were seeking to protect (the national umbrellas under which they were trying to hide their heinous crimes) were crumbling under the weight of intra and inter-state conflicts.

Africa, to borrow from the title of George Ayittey's book, had been betrayed by petty bourgeois clients. The voice of Nkrumah still vibrates in the inner chambers of Africa's collective memory. Fortunately, it echoes in the hearts and minds of the critical generation of African young men and women.

The new critical generation must drink from the deep fountains of indigenous Africa. And to succeed as a movement it must borrow strategies from the early African Youth movements of the 1930s and also exploit new opportunities that can guarantee democratic structures and a credible foundation for an African renaissance.

The early youth movements in the 1930s were imbued with a sense of patriotism and solidarity. The fire to free their people from oppression drove young people to create youth organisations as well as students' unions in which they militated and articulated the interest of Africans. Associations especially students' unions were Pan-African rather than the micro ethnic student unions that have flooded college and university campuses today. Their agendas were against any thing that stood on the way of African identity and solidarity. A good example is West African Students' Union (WASU) which was an important pressure group in the agitation against colonial rule and served as the training ground in militant nationalist politics for African youths studying in Britain. Most of the members of these associations were to become participants in various Pan-African congresses organised in the Diaspora. Then the young Africans were a collection of unknowns but soon they were to gain fame and assume political power in their different African countries.

After successfully pressuring for the pulling down of colonial flags on African soil, these young people became leaders with ostensibly a common purpose - to restore a sense of pride and dignity to their dehumanised people. Some of them succeeded but most went astray. Some of these leaders plugged all channels of protest and choice through intimidation and coercion. Some of the young intellectuals who wanted true independence and equal opportunities for their people - those who stood to protest against the misery of their people - were either forced into self-exile, jailed in underground prisons or killed in cold blood.

It soon became clear to most African youth that they would not be listened to in the one-party structures that dominated politics. They also realized that they could not express themselves freely outside the one-party systems. Thus, when they found that the structures of democracy were insulated to opposing views, some African youth opted to serve their nation through careers in the military. However, there too, some became brutal and autocratic military rulers while others used their military stature to open routes to democratic change.

The democratic avenues today, no matter how rudimentary, are more in place than they were immediately after independence. Multiparty politics is the order of the day in Africa today; hundreds of authentic and synthetic parties mushroom continuously. Freedom of the press is allowed though with a taint of symbolic or real censorship. Elections are now held giving people at least a possibility to choose whom they want even if they have no control over the election results. The constitutions are now reviewed not just by the President alone but also by a consultative committee or constituent assembly even if its members might be handpicked. The avenues are open. It is up to us to render them effective not by burning but by building, not by plotting but by planning, not through conflicts but through co-operation. We can only aspire for a real democracy when we listen to the voice of tolerance - not of victimisation.

There can be no democracy without the critical youths being in the vanguard and to be involved in the democratic process entails education. By education I am not referring to degrees earned in ivory tower academic institutions that produce narrow analytical minds. I am referring to the youths' ability to be cultivated in the respect of their society and tolerance for individual opinion. As the laboratory of Africa's democracy, youths, according to Dibussi Tande should be uncompromising critics of their socio-political environment. They should be instilled with a healthy scepticism towards values that might be accepted blindly. They should adopt a way of thinking that is contrary to all forms of monolithism without being carried away by the illusions and fantasies of pluralism. They should clearly say "No" to the utopia of their new demagogues wearing borrowed democratic robes (Tande, 1992). Equipped with such education the youths will have a vision that emphasises the force of argument, not the argument of force - a vision that turns obstacles into opportunities and stumbling blocks into stepping stones.

Every Generation has its Mission

Frantz Fanon rightly said that every generation has its mission - it either betrays it or fulfils it. African youths who are part of the critical generation must search for avenues to dream their own dreams. That is what I call "Youth Power". History has shown how young people have used youthful exuberance to effect reforms in their countries. It is through young people's protest that majority rule came to South Africa. The Sharpeville protest on March 21, 1960, left 69 young people dead. The Soweto uprising of June 16, 1976, saw 618 school children killed at the prime of their lives. Among the dead was Hector Peterson, a thirteen-year old school boy. The Sharpeville and Soweto uprising marked in a turning point in the struggle against apartheid. In Ghana, the young Flight

Lieutenant Jerry Rawlings successfully seized power in 1979 due, in part to demonstrations by student groups and pro-socialist student leaders. Throughout Africa, young people have shown that they are prepared to lay down their lives for democracy and, more often than not, their young blood has watered seeds of liberty.

Why then have the youths today taken to wine and leisure? Why has the present generation minimised its potential and capacity only to translate their ingenious energy into self-destruction? Why are the young people today perpetually eclipsed by the shadows of pent-up frustration and the penumbra of African aversion? Who is providing the young people today with tools of annihilation (guns, drugs, slavish models) instead of brains of creativity? This self-destruction must stop. Young Africans should know that their era of ploughing and sowing has come and that their progeny will not reap any harvest if the soil is left barren and effete. What I propose for young people who wish to overhaul their rustic democratic machinery is to come back to the strategy of pioneer Pan-Africanists which is "Think African, Implement National."
At the national level, youths should create broad-based associations, unions, NGO's, forums and movements that only they control and in which they can brainstorm, debate and look for solutions to the burning issues of their society. These groups should transcend ethnicity, Alma Maters, and other insular parochialism. Also, youth should get involved with grassroots organizations that seek to change communities positively. Grassroots organisations provide youth with access to the daily problems ordinary people face. These national associations should then be linked with continent-wide organizations. There are problems that are peculiar to the different African nations but a search for continental solutions is imperative in addressing the African malaise. The continent's chronic problems in the areas of good governance, human rights, conflict resolution

and economic development demand Pan-African solutions. We are not going to solve our problems through the escapist theory of brain drain but through the redemption theory of brain blend.

Addressing grassroots, national and continental problems allows youth to develop critical leadership qualities. The first generation of African leaders is either out of the corridors of power like Mandela, Kaunda, Senghor, Masire or out of the face of the earth like Nyerere, Nkrumah, Lumumba, Sekou Touré and Amadou Ahidjo. Africa now needs a new generation of leaders. Whether they like it or not, the mantle of leadership will be passed on to this generation. And this is where Olesugun Obasanjo's "African Leadership Forum" will be missed. Apparently in Africa, leaders are not groomed; leadership is simply thrust upon select individuals. The present generation is a mere hammock between Africa's betrayed past and its glorious future. Today's youths constitute the next generation to steer the ship of Africa. They are the generation to build bridges between the voices of the Nkrumah epoch and the vision of the Mandela era. But when they must have captured the reigns of power, will they remember the errors of those they criticised? Are some of them not running organisations or portraying leadership qualities with spasmodic fits of Mobutuism. Once in a position of power are they not going to perpetuate such a selfish circle of power jockey among themselves to the exclusion of a miserable population? Are they going to wallow in their fantasies of opulence and vanity? Are they going to place their personal egosystem over society's ecosystem? It is time to reconsider the politics of divide and dictate that have led to the cancer of chaos in our African countries. It is time they revisited our traditional democratic values that insist on the palaver theory, communitarian vision and collective responsibility. It is time we broke free from the paralysing chains of prebendalism and the humiliating bonds of neocolonial domination.

CHAPTER TWO
THE RISE AND FALL OF DEMOCRACY IN AFRICA

There is no universally agreed definition of democracy but its essential meaning is well understood. Simply put, it is maximum citizen participation in public affairs and accountability by the rulers. Chafe extends this definition by contending that the degree of involvement of the citizenry in the total affairs of their polity, within the standards of natural justice, determines the degree or democratic substance of a political system (Chafe, 1994: 132). While no clear-cut definition can be applied, there exist universal canons that make the presence of democracy felt in any society. Democracy is about defining power relations among all stakeholders in a given space. It entails the right to choose leadership, the right to protest against bad governance and the freedom of opinion and association. The right to choose leadership should be done freely and fairly, respecting the will of the majority. Such a leader must govern on the principles of equal opportunity for all, accountability and the improvement of economic welfare of the people.

When a leader manifests a style of governance that stifles economic growth and instead focuses on self-aggrandisement, it must bow to the voice of protest. For any society to progress, it needs to expose itself to the sunlight of debate - no matter how divergent the views. Debate requires two factors: ideology and tolerance. Debate is born on the premise that people have different ideas and vision of the society. Safety valves are therefore created to crystallise these ideas and vision into a nation-building process. Some of these valves are expressed through political parties, judiciary, legislature, press and the civil society. Their functions are to articulate the interest of the people and close the gap between those who govern and the masses. Every society must therefore seek to erect viable structures that can make democracy sustainable. To imagine that the mere presence of political parties in a society is tantamount to democracy can be very misleading. It is, unfortunately, in this trap that most African countries have fallen since the re-emergence of multiparty politics in the 1980's. The concession most leaders made to multiparty politics has not been followed by a conversion of the monolithic apparatus (constitution, mentality etc.). The body of the state was pluralistic while the engine remained monolithic and yet these leaders have been vaunted as being messiahs and apostles of democracy. Another danger we have been courting is the confusion between democracy and good governance. What sense does it make for a leader to be democratically elected by the euphoria of the ballot only for his governance to plunge the country in the abyss of economic stagnation? On the other hand, what would one make of a leader who gets to power "undemocratically" but succeeds in responding to the needs of his people? By extension, what does one make of an authoritarian rule that addresses basic bread and butter issues as opposed to a democratic regime that enslaves its people in the bondage of poverty? Elections, when carried out freely and fairly, are precursors of leadership but it is the vision of the leader that provides good governance. Elections provide the leader with popular vote and vision provides the leader with popular will. Therefore democracy and good governance must coexist.

Governance in Pre-Colonial Africa
While the creation of democratic models varies, the virtue of good governance is universal. By that token, democracy has always existed in Africa. It is as old as the Egyptian civilisation. Today it has been panel-beaten in some countries to suit the vision of either internal stakeholders or

external donors. As external donors, the West has insisted on multiparty democracy (Western liberal model) because it is born out of their culture. Any deviation from political party formation is regarded by the West as autocracy. That of course is fallacious. There must be an organic link between any model of democracy and the historical context of the society. In the precolonial Africa there were divergent opinions on state affairs without recourse to the formation of many political parties. Institutions existed that catered for dissenting views. According to George Ayittey, there were as many as four basic units of government in African societies that governed themselves. The first was the chief who was the central authority. The second was the inner or Privy Council, which advised the chief. The third was the council of elders and the fourth was the village assembly (Ayittey, 1992: 38). The duty of the inner, or Privy Council, was not only to keep the chief in touch with happenings in the tribe but also to keep a check on the chief's behaviour. It was more or less the judiciary. The Council of Elders had two functions: 1- to advise and assist the chief in the administration of the tribe, and 2- to prevent the chief from abusing his power. It was more or less the representative body of the commoners. At the village assemblies, the chief allowed the people to speak fully and freely until there was consensus. The majority opinion ruled if a consensus could not be reached - this was a cardinal issue on freedom of opinion. Although the chief was "in strict theory able to override the wishes of his people ... in practice he rarely ventured to do so because he knew the co-operation of the villages was essential for the successful government of the tribe. Therefore, real power lay with the people (Ayittey, 1992:40-42). Empires like the Mandinka, Bornu, Old Oyo, Sokoto Caliphate and Asante are examples of such indigenous African democratic institutions.

In societies where there was no monarchy, power was decentralised to allow the people to make decisions affecting their lives. No single person was responsible for all decision making for the group. Such societies practised co-operative leadership. What comes out of the pre-colonial African political system is that where decision making was not collective, like in some centralised states, decision making was not only consensual but checks and balances existed to trim the excesses of central authority. This democratic entitlement was further enhanced by a number of societal codes of conduct, or ideologies. First, our conception of power was distributive, not accumulative. Secondly, the society rested on the seminal concept of the traditional African family system (Ujamaa) in which the individual is regarded as part of a corporate group. In the same vein, there was nationalism in which the society was regarded as being greater than the individual and therefore concerns of economic sharing, collective security, fellow-feeling and even religious and racial tolerance were the hallmarks of our pre-colonial democracy. The consensus through dialogue concept called *Palaver Theory* was the subculture of the village assembly sitting under a tree and talking sincerely, listening actively, confronting creatively, and finally, building an agreement. Therefore, if nationalism, according to Walter Rodney, is a sense of oneness that emerges from social groups trying to control their environment and to defend their gains against competing groups then African nationalism had already gained ground in the pre-colonial Africa (Rodney, 1972: 242).

Impact of Colonialism
The question, therefore, is if Africa and Africans possessed such traditional yeast of democracy and nationalism, how is it that we still have not been able to bake the bread of human development and mould the cake of durable peace

in Africa? If, indeed, democratic entitlement is rooted in African culture, why do we continue to act as a conquered continent? Why are we behaving like a people under siege? The answer is at the doorstep of colonialism. When colonialism took Africa by its throat, it destroyed our indigenous political institutions and imposed on us the most autocratic and despicable rule ever witnessed in African history. Colonialists foisted on us a brand of civilisation that tended to uproot and alienate us from our traditional solidarity. They thought they had a divine mission to make us out of their images and consequently they let our development and model of governance be fashioned for their prime benefit. The Europeans regarded all attempts at development based on the African practical experience with contempt. They treated Africans as social inferiors incapable of governing themselves. Colonial exploitation varied from the most subtle indirect rule system of the British, the most controversial assimilation policy of the French, the most inhuman divide and rule policy of the Boers to the most sternly paternalistic tactic of the Belgians. No matter how benign or despotic the rule was, colonialism was meant to serve the interest of the metropolis. According to Walter Rodney, colonialism had only one hand - it was a one-armed bandit (Rodney, 1972: 223). Through these rituals of Christianity, commerce, colonialism and civilisation, Europeans crippled every aspect of our political, economic and cultural life. Monarchs who co-operated with the village assembly to hold community together, now decided to collaborate with colonial rule in sharing the spoils. Other monarchs who dared to resist colonial exploitation were either coerced into wars or dethroned ruthlessly. Societies that were held together by the fabrics of collective leadership were torn apart by new cultural stereotypes and transplanted political institutions. One major example is Burundi. Before the invasion by Belgium, society in present-day Burundi was divided among four ethnic groups: 1- BaHutu who were basically agriculturists, 2- BaTutsi (pastoralists), 3- BaTwa (pygmy hunters), and 4- BaGanwa (the royal clan). A common language (Kirundi), a common history and even a common belief system (Imana) united these groups. Theoretically, therefore, Burundi could be recognised as a tribe. According to Mworoha, Burundi's political leadership was derived from the royalty (Mwami or King), which proved vital in maintaining cohesion and peace in the society. The Mwami was surrounded by the "bashingantahe", a respectable group of elders chosen by the people to resolve conflicts within the community and to advise the Mwami. The mode of governance was based on dialogue and consultation known as ijambo (Mworoha, 1994: 174). The Belgians surfaced only to use the Mwami as a colonial agent not of serving the interest of the people, but of implementing their colonial agenda. The Belgian colonial historiography created social dislocation and ethnic animosities by legitimising the physical/social dichotomy between the BaHutu whom the Belgians described as leisure-loving and lazy and the BaTutsi whom they described as tall and intelligent. The Belgians did this by propagating the racial theory that the Tutsi were messiahs who had migrated from Egypt and Ethiopia and were endowed with leadership qualities, while the Hutu were timid and inferior people who owed their allegiance, obedience and servitude to the superior Tutsi (Mworoha, 1994: 175). This colonial myth created a status difference that led the groundwork for mutual distrust, ethnic confrontation and unabated massacres, which are now rocking Burundi. This is one of the many traditional societies torn to shreds by colonial invasion. Economic sharing which was a feature in pre-colonial Africa was transformed to economic dependency during colonialism. In all, colonialism deprived Africans of power. Power is the ultimate determinant in human society, being basic to the relations within any group and between groups, and when one society finds itself forced to relinquish power entirely to another society, that in itself is a form of underdevelopment (Rodney, 1972: 245). The agitation for independence was about the retransfer of power. It was then assumed that independence in Africa will transfer full powers from white rule to African rule. There was the African independence explosion in the 1960's but while all nationalists were legitimately concerned with seeking political kingdoms, most of them showed little ingenuity in seeking political structures that would make them genuine "Kings" in their newly found political kingdoms. They refused to see the traditional symmetry and rich ideological manure that was the substrata of pre-colonial governance. They hardly saw that the continent had much in its indigenous past to form the foundation of its democratic future (Mazrui, 1992: 9). The nationalists chanted hymns of anti-colonial nationalism without reviving melodies of pro-African nationalism. They spread the sermon of decolonisation without erecting the edifice of reconstruction. In the end, Independence brought along the euphoria of colonial departure without an agenda of indigenous arrival. On the other hand, had the colonialists any interest in leaving behind an authentic independent Africa they would have addressed four issues during transition conferences.

Firstly, *leadership*: who was to take the mantle of power? Would it be the traditional authority as it was in most of precolonial Africa or the newly educated elite whose nationalistic platitudes put them in the limelight?

Secondly, *ideology*: Even though the colonialists had eradicated the cream of our indigenous democratic culture, there were still vestiges from which the new "powercrats" would have borrowed. Were they compelled to inherit the colonial mentality that had institutionalised despotism to primitive heights?

Thirdly, *political institutions*: Did the apostles of independence have a free hand in choosing their future political structures without the paternalistic observation of the colonial masters?

Finally, *colonial boundaries*: Were the new leaders bound to accept Africa in its balkanised state or as a continental family?

These four issues might have been considerably addressed if the mode of transition from colonial rule to Independence was a carefully planned democratisation process, not one designed and guided by colonialists. Most of the transitional modes were remote controlled conferences that were half-hearted, rushed and chaotic (Nnoli, 1995). The result is that colonialism did not only leave a legacy of artificial frontiers and transplanted alien socio-political institution but the new "powercrats" (mainly the educated elites) accepted the colonial legacy - whether of frontiers or of bureaucratic dictatorship - on the rash assumption that they could master it, but instead, it mastered them. To these new leaders, "modernisation" meant the wholesale importation of non-African scenarios and solutions (Davidson, 1992: 182).

Julius Nyerere of Tanzania was one of the few leaders of that generation who shunned foreign ideas but instead instituted an innovative political experiment based on indigenous democratic concept. Nyerere's Ujamaa was a concept inspired by the traditional black African belief that people have an affinity to work, eat, produce and generally live together. Through Ujamaa efforts, Nyerere's government created co-operatives to boost productivity among community members and get all involved in some productive activity. That the concept was short-lived is another matter; that blames for its premature death have been apportioned to national impatience, state intervention and Western sabotage is another kettle of fish, but the important thing is that Nyerere refused to swallow the

25

strongly centralised and dictatorial economic structures of colonialism and chose to invent a concept rooted in his local environment.

Soon after independence most African nations adopted the one-party system. Arguably, proponents of this one party system drew inspiration from the precolonial "under the tree" discussion philosophy, but unlike the precolonial tree that entailed a bottom-up approach, a respect of divergent views leading to consensus, and a corporate and collective interest and responsibility, the one party experiment ushered a top-down approach, an intolerance and intimidation network and a personality-cult leadership. And so post independent structures like the legislature and the judiciary was pale shadows of the pre-colonial village assembly or inner Council. The system lacked any communication flow horizontally or vertically. The educated turned their backs on the masses only to connive with former colonialist in advancing a neo-colonial agenda. Even the traditional authority that would have reminded the new leadership of sane governance became accomplices. The jangling bells of independence now gave room to imperialism. Couched in pedantic political models borrowed from Britain, France, or America, the new leaders consolidated their positions of power for self-aggrandisement instead of popular participation. The society then went riot.

Economic sharing among the people gave way to economic individualism among the ruling elite. Traditional solidarity among the people was dismantled by the ruling elite and in its place, ethnic chauvinism was institutionalised. Societal concerns were substituted for sectarian interest and personal sacrifices were necessary only for economic gains. Africa, which began as a common geographical polity with shared values, saw itself walking down the road of continental destruction. The OAU charter did not help matters since leaders took refuge in Article III which called for "non-interference in the internal affairs of states and respect for the sovereignty and territorial integrity of each state and of its inalienable rights to independent existence."

Unable to restore Africa's indigenous soul in their national policies and hesitant to give Africa a united platform from which to launch its diplomatic offensive, another form of agitation began in the 1990s – the agitation for Democracy. If the wind of independence in the 60s blew for transfer of power from white rule to Africa rule, the wind of democracy in the 90s blew for the transfer of power from the coterie of ruling elite to the mass of industrious peasants. Africa was confronted with another transitional period in which the four issues that the colonial masters failed to address would come to the fore. Top among these four issues was the mode of transition which African countries needed in order to pursue their various democratic imperatives.

Unfortunately, as in the pre-independence era most of the African people were excluded in deciding the democratic apparatus their countries needed. Instead, multiparty democracy was propagated by those elite who had not been included in the "food-sharing" process and was imposed by the Western government through the Lord Judd's "carrots and stick" approach. Apart from a few countries like Benin, Mali, Congo, Gabon, Eritrea, Niger, Ethiopia and Zambia where participation was inclusive, other countries had multiparty basically by decree. Without any referendum, all fell into the trap of believing that multiparty politics was synonymous with democracy. As in the pre-independent era, little thought was given to indigenous institutions and to Africa's pre-colonial democratic culture. And, again as in the pre-independence era, the agitators did not set up an agenda for a united Africa but were concerned with individual national problems.

27

In the light of the above, it becomes clear that the history of liberation and agitation in Africa is one of protest without planning, of transitions of rule without transfer of power, and of national catharsis without continental empathy. Yet, inherent in this liberation is the search for an African soul. Caught in the frenzy that multiparty democracy was the panacea to our economic woes and political atrophy, by 1990 more than half of African countries had conscripted their people to the army of multiparty liberation. To be fair to multiparty advocates, they thought that this Western liberal model of democracy could usher in competition and mobilisation necessary for growth. It was presupposed that multipartism would give room to fair and free elections and that only the most competent persons would be leaders. It was assumed that the masses would be only mobilized to candidates whose ideological manifesto will bring them economic welfare and real political independence. But once again assumptions and reality were at loggerheads. In most cases, elections were neither free nor fair. The power of fraud gave advantage to those incumbent leaders who owned the machinery to organise and proclaim election results. Thus most of the elections held in Africa in 1990s did not turn the ebb and flow of power from the centre to the regions or from the ruling minority elite to the majority of masses. They were unable to transform the war of electoral victories into the peace of good governance and the stability of economic development.

That the so-called transitions to democracy were alien to the African soul can be seen in the names of the political movements that sought to mobilize the fickle and gullible masses desperate for change. Most of these parties adopted pedantic and Western-sounding names such as Social Democratic Party, Union for Democracy, Liberal Democratic front or Movement for Multiparty Democracy. Why not assume indigenous names such as Uhuru Party

28

(uhuru is the Swahili word for freedom), Bâ-fata Party (Bâ-fata in Mandinga-Guinea Bissau means the river is high and must be crossed). Such indigenous names spark meaning in the African context and are better understood by the masses. Identification was therefore bound to be on the basis of ethnicity, class, and sinecure. In fact most Opposition parties were set up without blueprints; instead invectives and rabble rousing were used to whip up the fickle sentiments of the masses.

But even where the opposition leaders took the mantle of power, the expectations have not been fulfilled. Of course, each country has its own balance sheet to give on the experiences of multipartism and their leaders are wont to give a positive balance sheet if for nothing else but to placate Western donors and the so called International Community. But the truth of the matter is that the only beneficiary of government policy must be the people. It is only the masses that are indicators of economic growth/development and structural stability in any country. No matter how much the IMF and the World Bank commend the effort of the ruling elite in economic issues, at the end of the day; it is the ordinary citizen who has the last word. Good governance must be guided by the will of the people. If the sporadic national uprisings and social dislocations are any measuring rods to political achievement in Africa then one can safely conclude that multiparty has been fashioned to serve the interest of the elite with an occasional spill over to the masses. Western liberal democracy as a model of governance has proved highly problematic when in operation in Africa not because Jacques Chirac said we are not yet ripe for democracy but because the history of Africa had not produced a society divided into social classes. As mentioned before, there was an erroneous conclusion that what divided the opposing groups was an ideological vision. Instead, they were divided in their search for economic space through political power. Second, the colonial dictatorial system had not been eliminated and all the independent leaders did was to add neo-colonial structures to already repressive systems - the call for democratisation therefore was hearkened to by-political liberalisation. Multiparty was regarded as a goal instead of a means. Stakeholders insisted on positions instead of interest. Multiparty was only seen as a step towards acceding power; the incumbent bent on maintaining it and the opposition bent on challenging it. And so valuable time, energy, money, life and property was wasted on elections that were done more out of convenience than conviction. The mere fact that Western governments have in some cases proposed the creation of new "governments of national unity" even after multiparty results were announced is testimony to the failure and futility of multiparty democracy in Africa and to the fact that the new input from multipartism is merely the expansion of the bourgeoisie space of misrule.

Multiparty hinges on the winner-takes-it-all syndrome, a policy of exclusion by itself quite unknown to the African culture that believes in shared interest and/or a policy of consensus. Because of the chaotic, reluctant and irrational way, the mode of transition was handled and the lack of consolidation of the democratic programme in multipartism, coup d'états have reared their ugly heads again since 1990. Indeed the pendulum of leadership in Africa today swings between the competing fraud of the ballot and the compelling force of the bullet.

Need for People-Centred African Unity
The transition to multiparty politics has dealt a severe blow to prospects for African unity. The political parties that scrambled for power in the multiparty era relegated the issues of intra African trade and continental unity to the background of their election propaganda. Hence, Africa, which began as one whole, gradually dissipated into

30

national cleavages and is now being fragmented into ethnic shells. The vision for a United Africa that was born out of the continent is becoming blurred within the continent. Never before have the stakes of African identity and survival been so high. And while Africa is being slaughtered in the abattoir of prebendal governance and neo-colonisation, Africans themselves are looking the other way. Yet, history is on our doorsteps again and we must give ourselves a transition. We have spent more than a century trying to let others think and act for us. Europeans and Americans have been carried away by their "providential wisdom" that political, economic, and cultural decisions cannot be made about Africa without prescriptions coming from Europe and America. Little doubt, therefore the development of Africa has always been closely linked to the interest of Western governments. An All African Peoples Congress comprising the main actors and valuable sectors in African politics is necessary now to assess the influence alien models have had on our lifestyle. This congress should be backed by a political will, good faith, patriotism and supra-nationalism. African countries should not precipitate their entry into any form of globalisation without defining and defending their own democratic and developmental agenda on the one hand, and creating viable strategies towards African unity on the other hand. While we chant the hymns of an anti-neo-colonial rhetoric, we must blast the thunderstorm of a pro Pan-African choice. The African democratic choice, as defined in the Tanzanian African charter for popular participation adopted in Arusha in 1990 and endorsed the same year by the Organisation of African Unity in Addis Ababa, is based on popular participation, the empowerment of the people, accountability, social and economic justice. According to King Moshoeshoe, an emerging political consciousness is in need of a culturally derived and defined African political and economic ideology which can be

31

culturally understood by Africans and so seen as dynamically relevant to their everyday problems and their own way of doing things. Any successful democracy capable of mobilising the people and of obtaining their co-operation, consent and active participation on the difficult road to African recovery, should be related to its own established, though now fragmented, cultural definition of African society (Moshoeshoe, 1992: 10).

Democracy is not the preserve of the West, nor a luxury of Africa. It is an ingredient that will continue to determine progress and development in Africa. For indeed, the fate of Africa will depend on how deep the seeds of popular participation and self-commitment are sown in the fertile African soil, and how well they are nourished and nurtured by the African people in tandem with their leaders.

CHAPTER THREE
MODELS FOR DEMOCRACY IN AFRICA

Two broad democratic choices of political systems remain open to African countries in their pursuit of democracy. They can either adhere to conservative models or adopt innovative choices. It must be stressed that the leadership of individual countries should make the choice after a national consultation through a kind of "indaba", "kgotla", "mbuza" or some other national forum that will bring together political, cultural and economic thinkers and planners across the national board. The decision (choice) made through this process would then have to be sanctioned by a free and fair national referendum.

Conservative Choice

Ideally, multipartism is based on peaceful competition among or between political parties with different ideologies and visions. This makes elections a cardinal instrument. In fact, a democratic political transition is deemed to have occurred if there exists a competitive election open to all potential participants, the administration of the election is free and fair, and all participants, including the losers, accept the results of the election (Bratton, 1999: 44). Multipartism allows the winning party to form a government according to its campaign promises while the loser acts as an alternative or watchdog. Other ingredients include freedom of speech, choice, association, rule of law and public accountability. Citizen participation is only crucial when the citizens can make choices based on ideology of the political actors.

Since the introduction of multiparty politics in Africa, two main power relations have been at play - the state and the political parties contending for power. Since it is the ordinary citizens who pay a great toll for this power struggle, a closer analysis of the positive and negative dimensions of this scenario is imperative. Such an examination reveals two scenarios, one in which the state is above partisan politics and another in which the state is paralysed by partisan politics. Each of these scenarios deserves closer attention.

Multiparty politics and state paralysis: This occurs in a highly bureaucratic and a largely centralized "multiparty" system. In spite of mass protests for effective democratization the leadership of the dominant political party engages only in cosmetic reforms that serve its interest, not that of the people. It pretends to relax its control on the political activities by opening up to pluralism but in effect still holds most of the decision-making powers. This is what Dr. Richard Joseph calls "Virtual democracy," and it occurs where autocratic regimes of whatever ideological complexion are encouraged to take a particular path when challenged to dismantle their authoritarian systems. This "stone or bone" choice is taken because established interests will not be threatened no matter the magnitude of upheavals. Most of these leaders only feign concession to the ideals of multipartism but in effect it is "concession without conversion" (West Africa, 1997: 1660).

In such a system, there is no democratisation, no decentralisation but mere administrative liberalisation. Whenever a state fails to decentralise, power becomes the source of rancour among parties. With no defined role between the party and state, the ruling party assumes all state responsibilities, sometimes, to the exclusion of citizen participation. Even the fashioning of the country's constitution becomes a matter of select status quo apologists who earn their living by "toeing the line." Because the state is irrationally centralised, the struggle for power is the only raison d'être for party politics. The state becomes a victim of the predatory ruling party and the aggressive opposing parties. The ruling party survives by depleting state resources. It is the state that provides funds for the running of the party and compensating party loyalists. Government appointees cease to work for the state and become stooges and sycophants to the blunders of the ruling party. The evidence is that before and during any elections state duties are abandoned as civil servants are plodding nooks and crannies for electoral campaigns. What finally emerges is a ruling elite interested in their self-perpetration. They arrogate to themselves the sanctity of truth and the monopoly of wisdom. And so they run down the throats of the masses their incredulous dogma of "national unity" and "national integration". Ruling party loyalty becomes synonymous with selfless patriotism. Opposition party sympathies are portrayed as foolhardiness and betrayal, and only traditional exorcism and career victimisation now serve as antidotes to "misled" opposition militants. Intimidation and intolerance become so rife that national cohesion is a pipe dream. Party symbols stand above national symbols and respect for party dogma is paramount to respect for state institutions. Since power is the bone of contention, elections are not only organised in rapid successions but also they take vital energy, time and resources that would have been channelled to development gains.

With the incumbent party's reluctance to establish a level playing field through a consensual electoral law and a neutral or impartial electoral commission, the winner of every election is predictably the ruling party. The result is, while the ruling party chants its stale victory song of continuity, the opposition embarks on widespread economic sabotage, social boycotts and structural instability. The opposition explores every avenue to bring disrepute to the state from international image tarnishing to national strikes. When it finds that getting to power is prevented by ruling power manipulation, the impatient, disgruntled and unfaithful opposition members jump out of the ranks to join the "government of national unity" actually a euphemism for a "club of national gluttons". Whenever multipartism descends to the abyss of the so-called "government of national unity", it often means that the country will either relapse to a one-party system or degenerate to repressive authoritarian rule. This is because in a "government of national unity" the ruling party seeks to stifle competition by either compensating or suffocating political opponents. Paradoxically, it is the same Western proponents of multipartism who are quick to prescribe the "government of national unity" model as a sedative after the multipartism they had earlier prescribed backfires. The fact is whenever the leadership of an incumbent party is forced to pay lip service to multipartism, the state is taken hostage. The state is pilfered and raped by the ruling party, and pillaged and plundered by the opposition parties. In the end the state becomes bankrupt and the IMF and World Bank come knocking with loans that come with draconian conditions. In the end, the ordinary people in the street who never enjoy the bounty of the state end up carrying the burden of the state's debts.

In conclusion, it is apparent that whenever the formulation of the county's vision is left solely in the hands of the party in power, the country is caught between the danger of tyranny and the risk of anarchy. Tyranny because, unable to benefit from the largesse of their labour, the masses are incited to see themselves as tribal cliques who can get the crumbs falling from the table only if they kow-tow to the ruling party. Thus, the people surrender power to the state and the ruling party. The dictum "I am the state" becomes "the party is the state". This is reflected in the arbitrary use of state power, state machinery, and state funds. In the process even the multiparty democracy system becomes distorted for personal or group gain (Nnoli, 1995: 21). Once the ruling party monopolizes power, it opens itself up to struggles for available power, to the detriment of national development. Nationalism is reduced to clientelism. The noble task of using multiparty democracy as an instrument for state building becomes unattainable with the masses bearing the brunt of state paralysis.

Multiparty Democracy and State Authority: Arguably, this is a preferable scenario to the one discussed above. In this case all citizens are ruled by a constitution that emphasises the respect of state institution above party politics. Democracy is seen as a means to an end. The development of the country is not absolutely related to party programmes but to decentralising state power and promoting appropriate values and attitudes that enable justice to be institutionalised in political relations. According to Okwudiba Nnoli, there are various aspects to the decentralisation of state power between the state and civil society. One involves the transfer of certain powers from the state to an emerging civil society. Another involves the decentralisation of power within the civil society. And yet, another aspect concerns the decentralisation of power within the state system itself. Decentralisation within the state system can be on geographical lines through federalism, on functional lines such as between the executive, legislative and judicial arms of government, and on popular sovereignty by subjecting the various organs of government to popular election by the people (Nnoli, 1995: 5).

The decentralisation of state power makes it neither repressive nor weak because state influence is felt from the centre to the regions. This also makes the state maintain its authority as one that represents the interest, and protects the rights, of all the citizens. Basic social amenities such as roads infrastructure, rural electrification, water installation, health, education and communication networks remain the preserve of the state and not instruments for sloganeering on behalf of those in power. The state formulates policies in these areas and parties seek only competent persons and credible ways of implementing them effectively so as to benefit the greatest number. In spite of party manifestos, the state takes responsibility in building a national cohesion through balanced development and the enforcement of the respect of state symbols - flag, pledge, and national anthem. In its pursuit of balanced development through a decentralised system, no region of the country is victimised for not being loyal to the ruling party or compensated for blind ruling party allegiance. The state authority provides a sense of community that is lost in the cleavages of multipartism. The line between the state and the party is enshrined in the constitution so that the ruling party does not feed on state resources. The role of civil servants, religious and security forces towards party adherence is re-examined. The media should not be polarised to the point where the state becomes ridiculed either through excessive image laundering or through an overdose of image tarnishing. Party symbols that run parallel to state symbols and are inimical to nationhood are abolished. Parties are identified by what they stand not meaningless symbols. Even in America (the flagship of Western liberal democracy) the Democratic and Republican parties are distinguished by their age long ideological tradition. In Africa, these ideologies should include among other things the party's vision for economic development, cultural reforms, rural development, fighting urban crime, creating employment, agricultural production, development of private the sector, regional integration in Africa and African unity.

One strength of this model is that the authoritative state acts as stabiliser of party divergences; above and beyond these party differences and conflict of interest lies an overreaching national loyalty for all citizens. This is not to say the state should become interventionist in all aspects of national life. Professions, labour unions, churches and the private sector should be free of state patronage. The role and status of opposition parties should be well defined in the constitution in such a manner that they see beyond the power horizon. They should not be regarded as irritating nuisances or democratic bluffs, but vibrant alternatives capable of dreaming their own national dreams. For example, in Mozambique, the ruling party gives the main opposition leader an honourable status during state ceremonies and guarantees him a state subsidy. This does not prevent him from making vitriolic criticism of the ruling party. In Botswana, the main opposition party does not wait for election time to unveil its reform package but persistently suggests ideas that the ruling party can advance for the betterment of the citizenry.

Another strength of the multiparty and state authority arrangement is that party politics do not undermine or compromise state responsibility. A good constitution is able to define the structure and function of the state, while the parties only make use of these constitutional provisions for the interest of the people. This arrangement closes the gulf between concrete programmes and mere improvisations, development and demagogy, political astuteness and political patronage. It provides a symbiotic relationship between party politics and state responsibility because roles are duly defined. It shifts emphasis from vain promise to concrete realisation of projects. It broadens the visionary scope of party politics, as politicians have to think hard for new development programs to include in their party manifestos and to woo membership. In the end, what multiparty and state authority alliance produces is a stable society governed by constitutional law in which a culture of tolerance, mutual respect, democracy and development coexist. It is above all, about a state that is authoritative without being authoritarian; one that places popular participation over competition, one that sets in course a mechanism that puts the nation first.

Innovative Choices

While African countries have been quick to adopt models from a conservative choice, models from an innovative choice have been in short supply in the market of political systems. The structural imposition of a colonial legacy, immediately after independence and the cultural brainwashing of the African educated elite, have accounted for the demise of innovative experiments. Yet, some of these experiments have been a recipe for stability and progress in Africa. Immediately after independence, Julius Nyerere of Tanzania and Milton Obote of Uganda understandably felt that their countries needed delicate, political, and electoral engineering to help them create a viable political order. While Nyerere's experiment will be discussed later, Milton Obote's vision of a parliamentary system was a break from the conservative Westminster model in a way. Obote insisted on making each Member of Parliament stand in four different constituencies - one in the north of the country, one in the South, one in the East and the fourth in the West. This design envisaged a situation in which every Member of Parliament would need to show allegiance to four different ethnic areas of the country. This multi-ethnic accountability in parliamentary life would force the candidate to develop positions and platforms which attempt to accommodate different groups rather than divide them. Between the elections every five years, each Member of Parliament would need to nurse four vastly different constituencies, and would, therefore, need to provide leadership in finding national perspectives on public issues rather than advocating narrower sectional and sectarian interests (Mazrui, 1986: 186). But, before this innovation model could take root, Obote was overthrown by General ldi Amin Dada. Amical Cabral, Tom Mboya, Thomas Sankara, and a host of African heroes were killed for daring to invent a future based on the African character. An innovative political system is all about the pursuit of the essential ingredients of democracy in ways that take full account of African circumstances, a democracy that is introspective in structure but could be universal in content.

Since independence, African countries have been grappling with various forms of government - most of them moulded from external thought - and the result has been grossly dismal. It is in aversion to those externally-inspired models that Jose Chipenda declared: "Since 1990, African countries have spent over one billion U.S dollars on the formation and servicing of multiparty democracies, with hardly any country emerging with a stable and mature multiparty system of governance" (Tam tam, 1996: 11). As the sun of hope rises, Africans should take a long and hard look at their borrowed and imposed political systems. They should not be scared or intimidated to try bold and assertive democratic alternatives that will lead Africa to the path of redemption and, hopefully, development. The reality today is not whether we as Africans have one, two, or one hundred or two hundred political parties. As Salim Salim Ahmed puts it: "What is important is, how really do we insulate and strengthen the culture of democracy in our society? How do we go about building the institutions, which underpin the democratic governments in our societies? How do we ensure that those who hold offices are accountable; that the standards of integrity are enhanced?" (*West Africa*, 1997: 299). It is in this regard that four models under the innovative choice are examined below.

Model One: Umbrella Democracy

Two parties and ideologies: This model entails the conceptualisation of two programs based on different ideologies prevailing in country. These programs are derived from an understanding of the country's needs and the ideologies are routes towards attaining these needs. These ideologies now find expression in two structures- either through a party platform or a list system. If it is within a party platform, the parties are named and the masses are obliged to identify themselves with any ideology that suits their perception about how the welfare of the people can be enhanced. Two currents of ideology often motivate reforms, that is the revolutionary (change) and the conservative (continuity).

Party A could therefore be called Revolutionary Party and Party B could be called Conservative Party. The concepts of Revolution and Conservative exist in the African psyche. It will therefore be necessary to translate these concepts by using local names of the parties. Political tags like Democratic, Reform and People's Party are obnoxious since all parties are supposed to be democratic, reform-minded and people-oriented. A proscription of party uniforms, banners and other symbols that accentuate party differences may be necessary. Symbols of parties could be reduced to mere traditional emblems and emphasis is laid on party manifesto. Party competition is limited to a two-horse race and it is assumed that civic education will help make political choices easy for voters.

General Ibrahim Babangida of Nigeria tried this experiment in 1992 when he created a transition programme. According to K. S. Chafe, the major salient features of this transition programme included the creation of two political parties by the government after it had decided that all the thirteen political associations that applied for registration were not qualified. The government did not only name the parties the Social Democratic Party (SDP) and the National Republican Convention (NRC) but their manifestos were also written for them by the government. Even their ideologies of a "little to the left" and a "little to the right", for the SDP and NRC respectively, were promulgated by the government "at the centre". All the finances of the parties were the responsibilities of the government through regular grants (Chafe, 1994: 138). This could be regarded as a programming of democracy from the top, but if well managed, can help introduce less divisive democratic practices in a young democracy. Unfortunately, the Babangida experiment in Nigeria turned out to be too government-interventionist and too full of power-scheming that it culminated in one of the saddest political outcomes the annulment of the results of what were seen as the fairest and freest elections in Nigeria and the incarceration Moshood Abiola who was heading for victory.

After a military coup d'état led by General Sani Abacha on 17 November 1993, Nigeria embarked on yet another innovative political system that was midwifed in a transition period. During this period, Abacha set up a 170 member committee of some of the most eminent and respected citizens, drawn from all facets of national endeavour, with a mission to chart a course that will ensure that by the year 2010, Nigeria will become a fairly developed country in the real sense of the word. Prior to the setting of the Vision 2010 Committee, Abacha had inaugurated another transition programme whose package was created by a constitutional conference. The constitutional conference acknowledged the failures of the British Parliamentary and American systems "because certain peculiar situations that are native to Nigeria were not taken into consideration" (*West Africa*, 1997: 515). Some of the innovative ideals proposed by the Constitutional Conference were:

43

a)   Sharing out and rotation of the major political offices in the country to six geo-political zones into which the country was partitioned. By so doing the fear of marginalisation and domination was put to rest;

b)   Local government elections were to be conducted on a non-partisan basis; and

c)   Five political parties were to be created and spread all over the country.

Other economic, social and cultural reforms were put in the package.

The slight departure from Babangida's experiment is that a broad-based constitutional conference was created to propose reforms for the country. This experiment would gain more credibility if those who took part in the reform package including the Head of the Transition period (Gen. Abacha), were to be barred from standing elections. It is also hoped that the manifestos of the five parties are the sum total of the different sensibilities that make up the society, not the personal conjectures of an overzealous group of politicians.

The strength of this experiment lies in the collective patriotism of the citizens and the individual astuteness of the political class. It lies in the ability to rekindle the flame of nationalism that will light the dark corners of the parochial cleavages. When one observes the number of parties that dwindle into oblivion before major elections, one is forced to reckon with the rationale behind this guided party's experiments. Elections have always been regarded as the ultimate raison-d'être of political parties and so prior to especially Presidential elections, there are two major labels: 1- Presidential majority consisting of parties which for various reasons support the incumbent regime and 2 the union of opposition consisting of a group of divided and discordant parties that hunger for change. This, in spite of the fact that the country's political landscape is initially littered with more than a hundred parties. But as time goes on, some parties fall on the wayside of poverty, internal crisis, bankruptcy of ideas, and cross-carpeting. In the end, only two sensibilities stand above the fray like in the old Western democracies of Britain and America.

The list system: The second manifestation of umbrella democracy is through what I refer to as the list system. Here, the state has a single party that we shall call Union Party. Union Party is now divided into Union Party - White List (UP - W) and Union Part - Green List (UP - G). While the party system depends on a sound program, the list system depends on competent personalities. More so, when the vision of a country has already been prescribed at the national forum, enshrined in the constitution and disseminated through a decentralised structure, all that is necessary is to have competent persons to implement this vision at all levels of the society. The electoral list competition (local, regional and national) must bear representation to the components that constitute the country's history and geography. These cleavages may include ethnic, religious and linguistic tendencies. During elections, which must be bottom-up, the white list is pitted against the green list and while the winner list governs, the loser list acts as a watchdog.

In 1964, Julius Nyerere found out that there was little or no opposition for his Tanganyika African National Union (TANU) in Parliament. In the face of such a massive national consensus, Nyerere understandably argued that it was a mockery to insist on a multiparty formula. A commission was appointed to investigate how best to achieve the democratic principle of choice under the umbrella of a single party. The commission affirmed the principle of a single party but linked it every five years to an electoral competition among members of the same party, with the people choosing from different candidates at election time. The constitution of Tanganyika underwent a change to meet this innovation (Mazrui, 1986:185). Tanganyika was therefore, technically, not a one-party state but a country with two single-party systems, divided by list platform and parallel to each other.

In Cameroon, all parties merged in 1966 to form a lone party called the Cameroon National Union (C. N. U.). The C.N.U. with motto "Union, Truth and Democracy" was coined "Party of the masses" ostensibly because it was a party based on the role played by its militants in the life of the nation, a party which listened to the masses, who, alone, gave it a force to accomplish great achievements" (C.N.U. Militant's Guide, 1976: 7). The pyramidal structure of the party (cell, branch, sub-section and section) gave a semblance of administrative decentralisation. Further administrative liberalism was noticed in the separation of party roles among the youths (Y.C.N.U.), women (W.C.N.U.) from the main party (C.N.U.). However, and in sharp contrast with the Tanzanian experience where there were two lists at every electoral level, the C.N.U. embarked on an electoral procedure that defied the basic tenets of grassroots legitimacy and competitive democracy. In accordance with Article 32 of the General Regulations of the basic text, "Elections shall be held:

a)   by a uninominal ballot for a single candidate in the cases of President, Vice President, Secretaries and Treasurers; and

b)   by a majority list ballot for other members."

The party may have succeeded in mobilising the masses, but it failed in giving them choices and opportunities to vote competent and credible representatives within their organs. The democracy at the bottom was sometimes compromised by the authoritarian rule at the top. It was therefore proposed that the system of double list within the single party be instituted, but the political barons argued that such a system would only be an official and institutionalised encouragement of the formation of an antagonistic electoral clan whose actions, even after the elections, would have the gravest consequences for the life of the party - it would be a simple return, under cover of the same party, to the former system of merciless electoral war accompanied by the same train of corruption, accusations and bloody struggles. Apart from the electoral conflicts, it would be a preparation for the disintegration and inexorable suicide of the party (Joseph, 1978: 75 - 76).

In spite of this assertion, the climate for a two-list system in Cameroon was conducive within the single party as early as in 1969. As symbolised by the manifestations of two principal currents of thoughts in the party, that is hard-line and liberal wings. The liberal wings wanted progressive reforms such as the nomination of candidates for the various elections (including presidential) by the party congress instead of by the political bureau, the introduction of a two-list system and the abolition of the idea of one person holding the post of the president of the party and of the republic. A powerful and influential hard-liner wing decisively rejected all these reforms. The party became the property of these hard-liner democratic barons who called themselves the National Political Bureau. This bureau nominated candidates for popular elections at the lower levels and expelled members from the party in the event of a particularly serious misconduct (*C.N.U Constitution*, Article 59). With a lot of decision making power at the top of the party hierarchy, the cell which was the basic structure of the party was reduced to the ridiculous role of merely distributing resolutions, leaflets, and other party documents, in addition to civic training and political education of the members.

However, in spite of the inherent lack of competition within this party, the C.N.U succeeded in building a Cameroon nation and in consolidating achievements in the field of development. This was more so because the party relied on the holding of a congress every five years during which a development on general policy, economic, financial, cultural and social policies of the country were defined. This five-year development plan was able to promote balanced development in all areas of the country as well as minimise tribalism and all other forms of political strife. The thin dividing line (at least on paper) between the party and the state, helped to dilute administrative overlapping between party barons and government officials. The dichotomy was ensured through the party defining national guidance, the government taking measures to apply it and the administration expressing the measures as facts. The party and the state collaborated closely in the realisation of the legitimate aspirations of the people by each being the conscience of the other. The blueprint of the state was produced in each congress. The congress drew inspiration from its broad representation and diversified regional reports. These reports always reflected the economic, social and cultural problems of each territorial administration making work easier for nominated regional representatives to implement. The congress, indeed, was the epitome of consensual ideologies of the two tendencies.

At last, and paradoxically towards its abolition in 1985, the C.N.U introduced the principle of a competitive two-list system in Cameroon. That legacy was briefly experimented by another umbrella party, Cameroon People's Democratic Movement between 1985 and 1990, when a multiparty decree opened the floodgates of Western liberal democracy.

Even though the umbrella democracy could lead to unbridled intimidation, indoctrination, ruthless regression and persecution, the personalisation and pornography of power, as well as the stifling of dissenting voices, there were benefits in the pursuit of developmental policies, the drive towards a national goal and the establishment of structural stability within the society.

For the umbrella democracy to face the challenges of today, it must institute a two-list party electoral system, from the local to the national level, reverse the pyramidal flow of power to propagate the bottom-up approach, minimise, or simply abolish, superfluous bureaucratic organs that have so far institutionalised a club of "sacred cows," and finally encourage healthy and constructive debate. The life-long president of the C.N.U, Ahmadou Ahidjo, privately endorsed the notion of dissenting views (even though his was a high handed regime) by declaring that "Oppositions in tendency are suitable within the party for without criticism and self-criticism, no progress nor improvements are conceivable " (C.N.U Militants Guide, 9). A new umbrella democracy should foster the idea that power belongs to the people and those who seek power must consult the divine will of the people. It is only through the people's mandate that leadership can enjoy legitimacy. The creation of small, but influential, cartels, namely political bureau and central committees, which normally consist of people who inflate the President's ego, will breed more chaos.

Through Nyerere's model in Tanzania and the C.N.U experience in Cameroon, it is hoped that future experiments in the umbrella democracy will combine the elements of competition and mass mobilisation. It will be necessary to keep an eye on developmental gains while erecting sustainable political structures, and liberalising thoughts while pursuing the goals of national consensus and a collective vision.

Model Two: No Party Democracy

This approach involves the banning, or restriction, of party politics in favour of individual initiatives. Where parties exist, they function under restricted circumstances since all political exercises, whether on democracy or on the economy are carried out under a national political network. The philosophy of this national political network is spread through its decentralised structures all around the country to the extent that participatory democracy is achieved. It installs a power sharing mechanism between the elite and the masses, as opposed to multipartysm where power is mostly the preserve of the privileged. There are two main emphases in this network; 1) the existence of citizens to run for election on their individual merits rather than under their party canopies; and 2) the effective decentralisation of the decision-making process to grassroots structures.

No-party democracy is sometimes mistaken for the one- party system, but this innovative philosophy is a sharp contrast to the one-party system in that under a one-party state political participation is decided by a coterie of the "chosen few" while the political network encourages election from the lowest to the highest office in the country. Secondly, while the one-party state hardly accommodates dissenting views, the political network is all embracing across the ideological spectrum without compromising its designed goal.

Furthermore, decision-making in the one party state is often the passionate rhetoric of the ruling elite while the political network encourages a bottom-up approach. The political network has the advantage of healing the nation's wounds, enhancing political stability and inculcating through a revolutionary propaganda, a sense of self-reliance, peasant or people empowerment, cultural independence and national solidarity. In recent times, two charismatic leaders have stood out in the practice of the no-party democracy: Thomas Isidore Noel Sankara who implemented a new political network during his relatively short term of office as President of Burkina Faso (1983-1987), and Yoweri Kaguta Museveni who became

President of Uganda since 1986. Though both leaders came to power through the bullet rather than the ballot, they foisted a much-acclaimed innovative political philosophy on their country people. Yet, literature, on these icons of participatory democracy in Africa, has bordered more on their revolutionary style rather than the democratic content of their philosophy. The media and other bourgeois scholars have spent more time castigating these leaders for not implementing what they regard as the conventional model of democracy but, beyond and above these prejudices, the philosophies of Sankara and Museveni need to be closely examined.

Immediately after taking power in 1983, Thomas Sankara dissolved all political parties, instituted a political network called the National Council of the Revolution (N.C.R) and urged all the citizens to form Committees for the Defence of the Revolution (C.D.R.) in order to be locally empowered with the activities of this network. The basic purpose and main objective of the N.C.R was to defend the interests of the citizens and fulfil their aspirations toward liberty, democracy, genuine independence, integrity and economic, social as well as cultural renaissance (Samantha, 1988: 22). Targeted against imperialism and reactionary social forces (bourgeoisie), the network sought to empower the working class, peasants and the dispossessed (masses). Transported in radical revolutionary speeches, Sankara used this system to "dismantle the political and economic foundations laid by the petty bourgeois intelligentsia and forces of foreign oppression in order to construct a new society cleansed of all the ills that had kept the country in a state of poverty, economic and cultural backwardness" (Samantha, 1988: 33). This transfer of power and societal cleansing was to be around the C.D.Rs. The C.D.Rs were to be the representatives of revolutionary power in the villages, the urban neighbourhoods, and the work places. Within the C

D Rs, the people acquired not only the right to review the problems of their development, but also to participate in making decisions and carrying them out.

Structurally, therefore, the C.D.Rs were organs through which the people exercised local power derived from the central power, which was vested in the N.C.R. The N.C.R was the supreme power, except during sessions of the national congress. It was the leading organ of this entire structure, which was guided by the principle of democratic centralism. On the one hand, democratic centralism was based on the subordination of lower organs to higher ones, of which N.C.R was the highest. On the other hand, this centralism remained democratic since the principles of elections applied at all levels and the autonomy of the local organs was recognised regarding all questions under their jurisdiction, within the limits and according to the general directives drawn up by the higher body (Samantha, 1988: 45). The N.C.R conceived an agenda for the nation based on national security and economic development. Special emphasis was placed on promoting economic development (through agrarian reforms) of the different regions, encouraging economic exchange among them and resolving ethnic prejudices in a spirit of unity. N.C.R.'s policy was therefore to unite all ethnic groups so that they could live in equality and enjoy equal opportunity for success.

Through the C.D.R.s, Sankara brought extensive reforms to the administrative, judicial, education and military systems. He restored a spirit of self-reliance and self-confidence akin to the Chinese, Korean and Indian revolutions. Through the no-party democracy, Sankara shifted emphasis from futile partisan elections to vibrant community development; from parochial power struggle to collective nation management; and from cultural imperialism to cultural integrity. The respect of the individual, love for patrimony and spirit of a local consumption pattern found in the average Burkinabe today is the result of seeds of Sankara sown some decades ago. He changed the country's name from Upper Volta to Burkina Faso - Land of Upright People.

He started where all patriotic leaders should start, i.e., changing the attitudes and transforming the mentality of his country people - not through political slogans, but through his own practical examples. Democracy, in whatever model, will continue to be blocked if people do not change their mentality of seeing themselves as a nation that can only survive through their own history. Real democracy lies in self-belief not self-hate and in cultural independence not cultural subjugation. It hinges on our ability to see progress, through our own eyes and development through our own parameters, of course, with due respect to the rule of law and human dignity.

Another no-party democracy network was instituted by Yoweri Kaguta Museveni when he came to power as head of state of Uganda in 1986. After inheriting a legacy of state bankruptcy, ethnic animosities and human rights abuse from the preceding regimes, Museveni restricted the functioning of party politics by establishing a political network called National Resistance Movement (N.R.M). The N.R.M's philosophy is developed on a rationalised and transparent administration, based on the concept of accountability and effective grassroots participation in the decision making process. It holds, among other things, a view that it does not have all the wisdom and that there is a need to be open-minded and to accept criticism (*The Courier*, No 141:23). The N.R.M. relies a great deal on its local governments called Resistance Councils (R.C.). The committees, which are built on a pyramidal and hierarchical structure, are spread all over the country, from the village base through parish, sub-county council, county-council and district levels. Regional development is fostered through these Councils.

This accounts for the rapid economic growth Uganda has enjoyed since the institution of this network.

As regards political parties, N.R.M. persuaded the political parties, principally the Democratic Party (D.P.) to agree to a power-sharing arrangement and the suspension of political activities for a couple of years. This led to the formation of a broad based government, but with individuals chosen on merit rather than on the basis of political parties, although nearly all the parties including the Uganda People's Congress (U.P.C), the most bitter opponent of the N R M, had members in it. So even though elections are conducted at all levels through a unique non-party system, the national government is made up of individuals from various political parties. Initially individuals were elected to parliament after winning through six stage (the first by direct election at the village level and by five different electoral colleges - it was then modified with members of parliament being elected directly instead of by a series of electoral colleges. Whichever way, the fact is that citizens are elected on their merit and not on party affiliation. All politics is therefore conducted through the political network.

The evolution of this National Resistance Movement has rescued Uganda from violence and upheaval as it is believed that small scale practical rebuilding at a grassroots level is mirrored in the tolerant, broad-based civilian and a military central administration. The N.R.M. system is credited to have brought a measure of political coherence and stability unknown in the country for a long time. It has given Uganda years of relative peace and stability, which have enabled it to tackle most effectively the economic rehabilitation programme it launched in 1987.

While visiting Uganda in December 1997, the then United States Assistant Secretary State for Africa Affairs, Susan Rice, told Voice of America that Uganda has one of the fastest economic growths in the world. The most spectacular strength of the no-party politics was recorded with the return of Ahmadou Toumani Toure as President of Mali in 2002. Toure campaigned and won the elections not under a party banner but in his own charisma and merit. How else, therefore, can we define democracy? Democracy is about who has the power, who controls the economic resources, who benefits from the country's wealth. It is about community development reminiscent of what happened during village meetings where each person, irrespective of their party line, or religious and material affiliations, placed the development of the village paramount. The villagers take control of the governance of their own community and take responsibility of its stability and equitable distribution of its resources. Sankara and Museveni have proven that these essential ingredients do not have to be expressed through political parties. Democracy therefore goes beyond election and the formation of political parties.

A no-party democracy operates on three levels:
1. the presence of a charismatic leader with a hero cult,
2. an indigenous national ideology; and
3. a decentralised participatory structure.

Without resorting to personality building, the no-party democracy must have a leader that communes with the rank and file. The masses must identify themselves with such a leader through loyalty to his vision and solidarity in development; the people must feel the humanness of their leader far from the magic aura of a demi-god. The leader himself must possess some authority in the control of the national ideology. He must be firm without being wicked. And fair without being weak. Democracy, without dictatorship, gives rise to anarchy; dictatorship without democracy gives rise to tyranny. Every good leader should blend Democracy and Dictatorship in the right proportion if good governance is to be achieved. Great civilisations have existed through hero cults like Che Guevera (an Argentinean) of Cuba, Mao Tse Tung of China, Abraham Lincoln of America, Winston Churchill of Britain, Charles de Gaulle of France, Lenin of Russia and Emperor Meiji of Japan. To these icons one must include Patrice Emery Lumumba of Congo, Amical Cabral of Guinea Bissau, Kwame Nkrumah of Ghana, Tom Mboya of Kenya, Abdul Nasser of Egypt, Murtala Mohammed of Nigeria, Um Nyobe of Cameroon, Muammar Gadaffi of Libya and Nelson Mandela of South Africa. These revolutionaries continue to savour the respect of the ordinary African because they dared to invent a future from a glorious past and an innovative present. Sankara and Museveni have joined those visionaries who have remained unruffled by the exigencies of Western liberal democracy, with its entire attendant futility and sterility.

As for national ideology, its indigenous ingredients include popular participation, self-reliance, self-confidence, distributive economics, stability and progress. These ingredients are packaged in a national movement that has roots in every nook and cranny of the country. An ideology cannot survive on mere political cant; it survives on an assertive pedagogic revolution. Whether in fiery oratory, symbolic gesture or structural transformation, this revolution seeks to de-colonise the minds and restore a form of traditional communalism. The revolution should pierce the hearts and consciences of citizens toward nation building, self-confidence and genuine independence. With a committed ideology, a revolution serves as a pact between the hero and the masses. Indeed great nations have been borne through revolution like the French revolution of 1789, to the Americans Revolution of 1823 and the Russian revolution of 1917. To these one must include the Burkina Faso revolution of 1983 and the Ugandan revolution of 1986. Such revolutions succeed when power is by the people, to the people and for the people. There must be emphasis on mass mobilisation instead of elite competition. Indeed the elite have been the bulwark of most democratic processes in Africa, since they confuse their personal interest for national interest and prefer ostentatious privileges to communal benefits. The elite will always favour a system with periodic elections because through it they can climb the slippery slopes of their predatory politics.

Since the quest for economic spoils is at the heart of the rat race for political struggle, democracy can be expanded only when the issue of bread and butter reaches those at the bottom of the political pyramid. Herein lies the third condition for a no party democracy - decentralised system that empowers local government and decision-making. For the indigenous ideology to spread regional committees must be left in the hands of the locals and development priority should be the preserve of the region. Like Basil Davidson puts it, "the key to the progress, even to survival, was not to be found merely in the multiplying of the party rivalries at the centres of the executive power, however much a structure rivalry might be desirable. It would be found, rather, in devolving executive power to a multiplicity of locally representative bodies. It would be found in re-establishing "vital inner links" within the fabric of society (Davidson, 1992: 294). Agreed, a no-party democracy has it dangers especially when the hero substitutes himself for the nation, when deliberation gives way to dictatorship, and when consensus is replaced with conformity. Yet, other countries have been allowed to develop their own democratic models, why should African countries suffer from the dictates of neo-colonial lessons? Why have those popular African heroes, who have insisted on trimming the gargantuan appetite of national elite and the inhuman exploitation of neo-colonialism been assassinated? Why have their heroic experiments at indigenous democracy been short-lived? Why have African leaders, who enjoy countrywide grassroots support, been stigmatised as terrorist or radicals by Western governments and their African lackeys? Why have the international community and their satellite tropical hypocrites paid lip service to African countries, which have recovered from war and have embarked on a reconstruction based on original home-grown democracy and development? Why have Africans themselves refused to believe in their own ingenuity and to protect their own revolutionaries? Until answers are provided to these questions, the search for peace and development in Africa will be as futile as the hullabaloo of globalisation and the rigmarole of international co-operation. The wind of change must be followed by the will to change and this will to change must be inspired by the realities of time and the vision of the people. Let the people alone have a say in how they want to be governed and a way in which they can reject their system of governance. Periodic conferences that asses the level of development, free debate on people's view of reforms and occasional referendums could be parameters to evaluate the people's desire for this system of democracy.

Model III. Consociational Democracy
An alternative to the current dogmatic proclamation and imposition of the multiparty model of democracy in sub-Saharan Africa is a model Canadian political scientist Almond and Verba refer to as Consociational Democracy. This term applies to a constitutional structure, which is canton-based, as in present day Switzerland. This federalist grassroots approach seems to correspond well to societies characterised by distinct ethnic cleavages and a fragmented socio-economic structure (Burgsdoff, 1992: 61). This model of democracy is based on three important principles. First, there is a restriction to party politics. Second, a specific ethnic group enjoys maximum autonomy with

respect to its day-to-day affairs - thus the direct responsibility of the people living in one distinct region is confined to that particular area. Thirdly, regarding representation at the federal/national level each ethnic group elects its own delegates or representatives. Matters of nationwide concern are decided at the federal level by the community delegates who make up, so to speak, the national government.

To help us understand how this model of democracy would work in an African situation, let us imagine a country with eight regions. Each region would have a local council comprising 50 members elected by direct suffrage but taking cognisance of proportional representation: These 50 members would then constitute an electoral college that elects, on proportional representation, 30 members to a regional assembly. Members of these regional assemblies form an electoral college to elect 10 members who then form the highest national decision making organ in country. This organ could be called the Federal (or national) Assembly. The end result is 80 members in the federal assembly, 240 members in the regional assemblies and 400 at the local government level.

The next task would be for the federal assembly to vote for a speaker, two deputy speakers and for ten members of the council of ministers. Each minister would carry out specified functions such as minister of health, minister of finance and so on. In this model, the title of president (so loved by many power-hungry politicians in Africa) could be avoided. The federal or national assembly becomes a people's body carryout national functions without the interference of partisan politics. Elections in this model could be held every five years with the possibility of rotating the highest posts among the country's eight regions. Because most of the decision-making process would be at the base (local government), the representatives depend directly on and are specifically answerable to their respective electorates.

Ethiopia came closest to the consociational democracy model after it adopted the 1994 constitution. On November 22, 1994 the constitutional assembly in Ethiopia came out with a provision which allowed for ten regions or Kilils, so drawn that each one of the main ethnic groups dominates. Considerable executive powers are in the hands of the Prime Minister even though there is a president. The Ethiopian experience recognises the existence of ethnicity and it is using the energy of its different people by creating autonomous self-governing regions. Ethiopia could go further and abolish the titles of "president" and "prime minister" and embark on extensive decentralisation within the regions.

African countries do not have to determine their regional jurisdiction only on the basis of ethnicity. It could be on linguistic, religious or geographical considerations. Most importantly these considerations should not compromise nationalism and a collective national vision. Depending on the defined regional jurisdiction, a country may have two, three and four regions with a region loosely defined as "a geographic zone populated by a distinct group of people sharing the same socio-cultural values, similar types of economic production and subsistence and adherence to a traditionally embedded system of political self-organisation." Let us not forget that in the Athenian city-state where democracy was first practised in the ancient world, the council of 500 which constituted the steering committee of the assembly was composed of 50 members drawn from each of the 10 tribes and that the board of magistrates comprising 10 members was also chosen on a tribal basis; Athens enjoyed peace and stability based on this consociational system before it was conquered by the Macedonians. For African countries with many tribes (most of which do not have permanent territorial limitations), it would be easier for regions to be demarcated through geographical convenience. However, whatever criteria are selected, Africans should understand that the blood that unites them is thicker than the artificial boundaries that may be created for administrative expediencies. Homogeneity is an ideal and the search for tolerance and accommodation should be the goal. But if the regions are haphazardly created; if there is no proportional representation in the regional assembly; if there is no respect for human/minority rights; if the fruits of regional autonomy are not equitably distributed; there will be agitation for the creations of other regions. All regions should therefore have their loyalties through their political self-organisations and economic interest than through their dispersed views of parochial solidarity.

Apart from the fact that consociational democracy reduces national election processes, Burgsdoff argues that this model not only enhances the community's ability to run their own affairs; it also minimises the risk of inter-ethnic conflicts as each group is in charge of its own political, cultural and economic spheres. (Burgsdoff, 1992: 62). According to Nicholas Ogbonna, the greatest advantage of this system is that with the possible exception of the grassroots level electorate, all the remaining electoral colleges are composed of literate voters who can use the benefits of their literacy to make a valid choice of suitable candidates. Furthermore, all manner of corruption which now characterises our electoral processes will be eliminated, or at least reduced to the barest minimum, because the system will be dealing with smaller numbers as one goes up from the base to the apex of a pyramid-like structure (West Africa, 1998: 62). Finally, given the characteristics of most sub-Saharan societies, a consociational model seems to provide an appropriate framework for democratic development and is more likely to exploit the traditional socio-cultural potential of African communities. (*The courier*, No 134: 3). This model can work with or without political parties. Where there are parties "The system will induce the emergency at national level of political parties formed through the coalition of regionally-based parties. This inevitably implies not only a process of negotiation but also a bottom-up approach to the establishment of national parties" (Oyowe, 1991: 72).

One of the dangers of consociational democracy is that extensive power may be given to the regions to the point of breeding ethno-nationalism - a recipe for secession. However the solution to secession is not to avoid it but to confront it. As an example, the Ethiopian constitution enshrines the right to any region to secede as long as 61 percent of the members of the regional assembly concerned agree. Three years later, a referendum is carried out in the region by the central administration (federal assembly, or people's body). Even with such a protective clause, there will always be professional agitators who would couch their vaulting ambitions under regional interest. Such clause should only send warning signals to the Federal Administration not to marginalise the regions in economic and decision-making issues.

Another danger is for regions to still look up to the federal administration for their own share of the "national cake". Self-government loses its essence when it relies more on sharing instead of baking the national cake. Consociational democracy can only be meaningful if the regions generate their own income to sustain their basic needs. It would be contradictory for regions hankering for administrative autonomy to turn round and depend entirely on the Federal Administration for financial support. While the federal administration should apply the law of derivation, regions should be industrious, ingenious and innovative enough to rely on their own productive capacities, consumption pattern as well as on their ability to harness their rich local cultural pools and mineral resources. To stem the ebb of ethnic chauvinism and promote the flow of ethnic co-operation, effective trade and communication system should be established among the regions. It is the sum-total of regional contribution that accounts for the national wealth; it is the cross-fertilisation of regional interests that accounts for national interest; it is the horizontal and vertical sense of belonging among the regions that strikes the chord of national unity. Any other national symbol foisted on the collective will of the regions will result in a loss of nationalism and a retreat to ethnicity. Only responsible leadership, healthy competition, genuine co-operation and economic planning can marry consociational democracy with autocentric development. Whenever a country succeeds in building its democracy on its indigenous political system, the citizens should focus on development matters.

African countries cannot continue to try democratic models at the expense of development. After all, even under authoritarian rule, some countries excelled on bread and butter issues; others have wasted valuable time, money and energy, changing governments, conducting local, legislative, presidential elections without producing sound economic results (forget about IMF flattery). In all, what consociational democracy seems to portray is that African countries already have natural constituencies on which indigenous democracy can be built.

Model IV: Monarchical Democracy

Precolonial Africa was replete with thriving kingdoms and chiefdoms many of which saw their demise during the colonial invasion. Where they survived colonization, the powers of the monarch were so diminished that allegiance, loyalty and submission to royal authority was severely compromised. In most cases, these traditional establishments became mere appendages of the "modern" political systems of post-colonial Africa. To make things worse, in many cases traditional rulers have compromised their own position by meddling in partisan politics. Ideally, traditional leaders should be non-partisan since their role is to serve their subjects irrespective of prevailing political cleavages; running for or supporting a particular party is therefore anathema. Also, traditional rulers should be loyal to the nation-state and constitution, even if they must occasionally question the behaviour of political leaders. In most cases the element of consultation and consensus should guide government-monarchy relations. Unfortunately, in most cases traditional leaders have flouted these principles and aligned themselves blindly with moribund regimes for self-interest.

Yet, according to George Ayittey, the traditional African rulers performed many critical functions. First, as the political head of the tribe, a king or chief was responsible for maintaining good order, handling public affairs and acting as the ultimate authority in all matters affecting the welfare of the states. Second, he presided over the chief's court, which was the final court of appeal unless there was a king, in which case his court was final. Third, he was the religious head of the tribe, the presumed direct living representative of the ancestral spirits that guarded the tribe and whose goodwill and co-operation were considered essential to the everyday existence of the tribe (Ayittey, 1992: 43). Therefore, despite the fact that the credibility of traditional rulers is undermined by their complicity in the slave trade, their selling out of their own people and territories to colonial powers and their passive (or compromised) role in the malaise of post-colonial Africa, kings and chiefs still have an important role to play in nation-building in Africa. The three possible roles are: 1- the king as ruler; 2- the king as supervisor; 3- the king as power-sharer. But before we delve into these roles, there are certain qualities that should be innate to traditional leadership. The traditional authority should be non-partisan since their role is to serve the citizens irrespective of the social cleavages; running for or supporting a particular party is anathema. The authority should be loyal to the state and the constitution even if they must occasionally question accountability and governance of political leaders. In most cases the element of consultation and consensus should guide government and monarchy. The autocratic role that is fast becoming a norm among traditional leaders should now give way to governance by the will of the people. Traditional leaders have sometimes flouted the principle of being spokespersons of their people as they align themselves with moribund regimes for self-interest. Under the traditional system of government there were two main factors that generally made it unthinkable and unfeasible for the chief to impose his will on his people. First, his sacred duty as the link between man and his ancestors did not permit him to oppress his people and expect the blessing or cooperation of his ancestral spirits. Second, any dictatorial tendency would bring shame to his lineage (Ayittey 1992:46).

Today the memories of the complicity between chiefs and slave masters/colonialists have compounded the eroding status of traditional power. The result is that traditional authority is being regarded with contempt and disdain. The challenge today is for chiefs to rediscover their sacred authority and traditional roles by establishing a covenant with their people. They must capture the spirit of nation building by acting as mediators of disputes, repositories of ancestral worship and catalysts of community development. This can be achieved in the following roles:

The King as ruler: One of the few kingdoms in Africa in which the king is still a ruler with considerable executive powers is Swaziland. The Swaziland monarchy was established several centuries ago. King Sobhuza I became head of state in 1968 when colonial rule ended.

Under Sobhuza's rule, there was absolute monarchy in which legislative and executive powers were vested in the king. After the fall of Sobhuza, King Mswati III took over as a constitutional monarch in 1986 and disbanded the liqoqo (traditional advisory body) and replaced it with a traditional system of administration called tinkhundla, which means a centre where people meet (Nxumalo, 1994). The tinkhundla arrangement seeks to decentralise power to the people. However, in spite of Mswati's major departure from monarchical despotism, pressures for democratic reforms compelled him to appoint a consultation committee to sound out public opinion. The committee created in 1990 travelled round the country receiving submissions and holding public meetings. It reported back in February 1992 that the majority of the people wanted to see a more democratic system established in Swaziland. The king then set up a Constitutional Review Commission to determine the kind of changes they wanted. Within months the commission reported that there was widespread support for tinkhundla but also demand for a parliament elected directly by the people through a secret ballot system (*The Courier* 1994: 25). The result is that at the time of this writing Swaziland had a dual form of government - the monarchy representing the traditional system and a modern parliamentary structure modelled along Westminster lines. The 1972 ban on political parties has not been lifted because the Constitutional Review Commission provided enough evidence that the multiparty system lacked popular support and was considered a recipe for division and disorder. Another credit to Swaziland's monarchical democracy is the fact that it allows for strong civil society organizations such as the People's United Democratic Movement (PUDEMO), the Swaziland Youth Congress (SWAYOCO) and the Human Rights Association of Swaziland (HUMARAS) which are openly critical of government actions.

However, Swaziland still struggles with an uneasy relationship between traditionalist (those for monarchical democracy) and modernist (those for multiparty democracy) primarily because the role of the King has not been thoroughly defined in the constitution. The power of royal authority over most facets of government life is still unquestionable. A harmonious relationship between traditional rule and the modern state requires that Swazis address and explore three issues. Firstly, can/does the tinkhundla system really allow for free and fair competition as well as decision-making at the local levels? If this is possible then argument for a "modern" parliamentary system could be weakened. Secondly, and on the other hand, can/does the bicameral parliament (which is now elected directly on a secret ballot basis) become a centre of progressive debate, aimed at development issues rather than power struggles? Then, the traditionalists' fear that competitive politics would foster political cleavages and stagnate national development could be allayed. Thirdly, and finally, the power struggle between the king (Ngwenyema, Swazi for lion) and the queen mother (Indlovukasi, Swazi for female elephant) should be resolved constitutionally. The constitution should make it clear that the King is the head of state, not other members of the royal family.

The way I see it, Swaziland is better off remaining a monarchical democracy in which the king rules. The experiences of other African countries that became "multiparty democracies" in the 1990s make it clear that it is an illusion to think that adopting a multiparty model of democracy represents progress. An effective monarchical democracy can be built around the traditional tinkhundla system with or without an elected parliament. Alternatively, the king could remain ruler but let parliament take a leading role in national decision-making. The position of prime minister could be abolished. The king would appoint the speaker of the national assembly from the elected Members of Parliament. The speaker becomes the link between the people and the king. A cabinet could also be created by appointments or elected from among the members of parliament. The Swazi generally love and respect their traditions and traditional rulers and there is no reason why they cannot pursue a policy of political and economic empowerment of masses within the boundaries of their traditions and culture.

The king as supervisor: The other example of a monarchical democracy in Black Africa is Lesotho. Here, the king is not ruler but a supervisor - making sure there is good governance of his subjects. While the king of Swaziland retains considerable executive power, the king of Lesotho has relinquished most of his power to the Prime Minister and the cabinet. Lesotho's history has seen an oscillation of power between the monarchy and an elected Prime Minister. During colonial rule the king had executive powers even though he had to consult with a British-appointed Basutoland Council. At the end of colonial rule in 1966, executive powers effectively passed to the prime minister whose authority was based on commanding a majority of the assembly (Moroney, 1989: 270). Between 1966-1985, the powers of the prime minister increased while those of the king were merely ceremonial. But following the military coup of January 1986 returned executive and legislative powers to the office of the king. He was supposed to be advised by a military council and the council of ministers. However, the relationship between the palace and the military deteriorated to such an extent that the king (then King Moshoeshoe II) was forced into exile. His young son, David Letsie III, replaced him. On August 17, 1994, King Letsie III suspended the constitution and dismissed the head of the government, accusing him of dictatorial behaviour. This constitutional crisis, however, was short-lived as the roles of the monarchy and the prime minister were delineated. The Prime Pinister handles executive matters; the king stays out of politics. The result is a political system in Lesotho now, in which the king is ceremonial figure, while the executive powers are with the prime minister.

However, Lesotho, like Swaziland still has issues to resolve. It is desirable that the separation of power between the monarchy and elected officials be fully enshrined in the country's constitution. The status and role of the king, of the prime minister and the bicameral national assembly, (especially the senate in which some members are appointed by the king) have to be further clarified. Also the role of multiple political parties should be scrutinized. Currently, the country operates along a quasi-multiparty arrangement in which, even the veteran opposition leader, Sekongane, acknowledges that there is no significant ideological divide since the ruling party and the opposition are committed to developing their country. (*The Courier*, 1995: 42). Perhaps, rather than having Western-style competing political parties, Lesotho could revive its traditional "Lekhotla," the non-partisan or community parliaments where local and national matters are discussed collectively and with shared wisdom. This traditional approach to resolving national issues may be better than a modern parliament that is simply a forum for power struggles. Finally, Lesotho has to resolve the role of the military in politics and stop its sporadic intervention in national politics. As I will argue later in this chapter, Lesotho, like most African countries hardly needs a standing army and should consider dissolving the military and replacing with a well-equipped and trained police force.

Power-sharing with traditional rulers: The third approach to monarchical democracy is one in which the king or chief shares power with elected officials. For example, a House of Chiefs can be constituted and granted decision-making powers that are binding to the state. Though the House of Chiefs would stay clear of partisan politics, it would be a force to be taken seriously by those in power. For too long now, House of Chiefs have been sterile and toothless institutions used as rubber stamp by those in power. But in this arrangement, the House would have an independent ideology and perception of national life. This independent vision is meant to infuse executive decisions with grassroots realities. This is particularly true because traditional rulers relate on a daily basis with the people and know their basic needs.

Another power-sharing design could be including chiefs in some of the decision-making political institutions of the country. For example, Cameroon's 1996 constitution includes a clause that calls for "representatives of traditional rulers [to be] elected by their peers" in the regional legislative bodies (*African Star Magazine*, 1996: 61). Another possibility is to include traditional rulers in commission and councils that oversee the electoral process, human rights etc.

Cultural Role of Traditional Rulers

Apart from the political roles discussed above, traditional leaders should also be seen as guardians of African traditions and culture. Traditional leaders should be appreciated as cultural assets critical to the resurrection of the African values that have been lost in the search for modernisation. In this regard, there are some promising trends. In Uganda, for example, the Kabaka is given respect during political events but his role remains purely cultural. In Ghana, Jerry Rawlings revived the cultural importance of the Asantehene and the traditional authority of chiefs especially through the celebration of the Golden Stool. According to the Asante mythology, the Golden Stool (Sika Dwa) descended from the sky and provided the Asante with a powerful means of cohesion (Davidson,

1993: 72). No one is allowed to sit on the stool. The annual "odwira" or yam festival held in Ghana recognises the supremacy of the Golden Stool and helps relate Ghana's political present to its cultural past. The President's involvement blends the spirit of traditional authority with the essence of contemporary executive power.

Monarchical Democracy and the Future of Africa

Monarchical democracy gives modern African states an opportunity to be shaped and inspired by their own native histories, cultures and pre-colonial political systems. This is much better than the scenario that prevailed in the 1960s when "old states [were] being swallowed entirely into new states as though these new states [had] never existed, save as quaint survival from the 'savage backwoods' of deplorable past" (Davidson, 1993: 188). Monarchical democracy could also help resolve some contemporary conflicts in Africa. Burundi, for example, could benefit from the restoration of its monarchy, which maintained stability and cohesion between the ethnic groups in pre-colonial years. It was the preferential practices of the Belgian colonial authorities and early missionaries that fuelled the polarization of the Kirundi-speaking people into the Hutu and Tutsi dichotomy. The abolition of the monarchy in 1966, the reintroduction of party politics first in 1989; then in 1993, further widened this dichotomy. Parties were founded basically on ethnic lines. Naturally the Hutu-dominated party had a permanent majority and the Tutsi party had a permanent minority. In other words, the stability fostered in Burundi by the monarchy was swept away by colonization and, more recently, by haphazard multiparty democracy experiments.

The restoration of the monarchy in Burundi could be done in this way. A Mwami (king) would come from the Ganwa - the tribe that historically represents royalty in

Burundi. The Mwami would then constitute a Bashingatahe, an inner council drawn from the four tribes to advise the king. The Mwami and Bashingatahe would only have a ceremonial, supervisory and advisory role over a duly elected national assembly or parliament. Eligibility to this assembly would not be partisan; rather, it would be based on individual merit and proportional representation of the four tribes with elections done by universal suffrage. Monarchical democracy, especially in bi-ethnic polarised societies like Burundi, can best operate under a no-party system. The assembly should then constitute an electoral college to vote the speaker and deputy speaker. The speaker and vice would be running mates drawn from the Hutu and Tutsi groups with the possibility of alternating the post between them. The assembly would then elect a limited number of parliamentarians as heads of committees. The heads of parliamentary committees would ensure that the terms of reference for their committees such as education, health and foreign affairs etc. are scrupulously implemented. This is an innovative substitute for cabinet ministers. The speaker and deputy speaker together with heads of parliamentary committee would be vested with executive powers while the assembly would retain legislative powers. The provinces, which form local governments, should have a governor and deputy running on the same Hutu/Tutsi formula applied to the speaker and deputy speaker of parliament. Meanwhile, members of the provincial and local council would be on proportional representation with considerable power at this local level. There may be a need to redraw provincial boundaries to accommodate national integration or ethnic tolerance.

I did not set out to prescribe a constitutional formula for any country. The challenge for African political scientists and constitutional experts is how to tailor their constitutional visions to the local realities and historical context of the African continent. The people of

Africa hunger for a democratic apparatus whose content is not tied to the spring or summer prisms of Western liberal dictate. They are tired of political systems steeped in arrogant and pedantic nomenclatures of Western political science. While it is acceptable that there are universal parameters of democratic practices, African should not lose sight of the paradox that the same Western governments exploiting the gullibility of Africans to graft Western models onto their political institutions, that these same governments who have refused to see an organic link between democracy and history remain conservative to their democratic models which evolved from their own history. The United Kingdom has remained a constitutional monarchy since 1689, France, a unitary Presidential system since 1958 (after a lot of botched political experiments), America, a federal Presidential system since 1789 (when U.S. constitution came to force). Therefore, Africans must have the audacity to build democratic systems informed by its own history and culture.

The Military and Democracy in Africa

This chapter on democracy in Africa cannot be complete without addressing the critical question of the role of the military in politics. So much ink has already flowed on the role the military should play in the democratic process in Africa. But one position that has not been made loud and clear is that the military has no role to play in African democracies. Traditionally, the military's role is to defend the nation against external aggression. Even when there are internal wrangles and splits in the nation's political life, the military as an apolitical and non-partisan institution remains in the barracks. Unfortunately, in this regard, the military in Africa has a horrible record. What wars have national armies fought apart from the wars against their own people? What defence have the national armies given their territories apart from the defence of the interests of the ruling cabal? Incumbent dictators stall democratic change by using soldiers to repress calls for change. The military persecutes prominent opposition leaders and wreaks havoc to civil society organizations. Sometimes a section of the military is metamorphosed into a highly favoured unit that is close to the incumbent head of state. This, so-called Presidential Guard benefits from perpetuating the anti-democratic principles of its paymaster. These units have an unflinching allegiance to the individual in power - not to the constitution or to law and order- and each time they unleash their pogrom on the unarmed army of protesters, limbs and lives are buried in a mire of blood.

Furthermore, the military in Africa exploits the least social or political confusion to transfer their professional idleness and brazen drunkenness into an orgy of looting, rape and murder of innocent citizens. The military uses fallacious reasons to get through the bullet, what they cannot get through the ballot. Some of these reasons include total marginalisation in social and security matters, cutbacks in their budgets, their slow advancement in the hierarchy. In a nutshell, every threat to their own corporate existence triggers their intervention in the political process. In May 1997, the military in Sierra Leone deposed a dully elected head of state basically because they felt they had been marginalised in favour of a foreign security network and traditional hunters cum private militia called "Kamajors". In Nigeria, fears that an incoming democratic government would scrutinise the corruption and human rights follies of the military under the Babaginda regime, and by extension the Abacha government, may have triggered the decision to derail Moshood Abiola's electoral victory of June 12, 1993 (Chege, 1995: 15). In Lesotho, attempts by sections of the military to destabilise the government in 1994, arose from the perception that the

74

civilian government was insensitive to corporate military grievances and the fear of a diminished role for the military in government. The August 1994 coup in the Gambia began as a demonstration of grievances over payment of soldiers' salaries and benefits by the Jawara governments (Chege, 1995: 14).

Wole Soyinka speaks for many when he describes the role of the military in African politics as being synonymous with "ignoble and retrogressive... wastrel, unaccounted for spending ... alienated apprehension of society and nationhood and ... brutal repression of civic aspirations" (Soyinka, 1996: 136).

On the other hand, it is important to mention that there have been situations where the military has intervened in politics not for their own self-interest but for the good of the nation. There have been times in Africa's chequered history, when the military has rallied behind the people to stop the political carnage, financial impropriety, ideological bankruptcy, and the pornography of power that had characterised certain civilian regimes. When the political compass of the country has instead pointed Westwards and "stomach-wards," the army has reoriented the country's destiny towards people-centred development. When the people's dignity has been crushed by civilian despotism, the army has sometimes intervened to restore the people's confidence. When the tyranny of civilian regime, has resulted in the suffering of the masses, the discipline of military regime has thawed, the ice of disillusionment.

Military interventions in Africa have sometimes served as stabilisers of political crisis and damage control agents of civilian excesses. The colossal achievements of General Murtala Mohammed of Nigeria just in nine months of power cannot be narrated here. His tenure of office was one of stability, discipline and economic advancement in Nigeria, and one that laid the foundations for the return to civilian government in 1979. Captain Thomas Sankara's four year stint (1983-1987) as Head of State of Burkina Faso remains the most revolutionary, progressive and developmental for a country that had retreated to the backyard of economic stagnation and for a people that had cultivated a culture of self-hate and self-denial. Museveni's guerrilla intervention in the democratic masquerade of Obote's Uganda in 1986 has brought solace, stability and economic growth to the nation. General Amadou Toumani Toure, Head of State of the transition government of Mali (1991-1992) gave his country a new lease of life by laying a solid democratic foundation for multiparty democracy. One cannot undermine the relative achievement of Colonel Gaddafi of Libya, Jerry Rawlings of Ghana and even with all the tyrannical transgressions that the military regime of General Sani Abacha of Nigeria committed, the General may still be granted political penance for equipping Nigeria with a Vision 2010.

In other words, Africa has had civilian saints and civilian devils in the same way that it has had military heroes and military villains. Africa has been shelter to civilian vultures and military vampires as well as civilian doves and military troubleshooters. Africa has sometimes been haunted by the nightmare of civilian dictatorship only to be harassed by the eternal transition of military kleptocracy. On the other hand, the short dawn of military reforms has sometimes been followed by the long dusk of civilian anarchy.

It may be for these reasons that some scholars have advanced ideas intended to reform the military and help it to contribute toward building democratic societies in Africa. However, my position is that any leadership that is not based on the free and fair mandate of the people lacks both legitimacy and legality. Leadership derives its strength from the popular will of the people and the people must be allowed to manifest this will through the transparency of the ballot box. "A military regime no matter how benevolent is a far cry from a democratically elected one" (Arifalo, 1982: 161).

If there is a diminished professional role for the military as defenders of the national territory—in the light of peaceful resolutions to interstate conflicts—and no legitimate role for the military in politics, then my proposition is that African states must dissolve their military establishment and replace them with a vocational, well-trained and equipped police who would maintain law and order and create an environment suitable for economic development and democratic governance. The abolition of the military and the professionalization of police would be a decisive milestone in Africa's search for security, political stability and economic development. It would turn the continent's weapons of destruction into tools for production.

CHAPTER FOUR
STRATEGIES FOR AFRICAN UNION

It is ironic that the very Western countries that stabbed and derailed Nkrumah's vision for African unity have now grouped together to form a European Union. The end of the geopolitics of the cold war has confirmed that the United Nations is little more than a snowball of the United States. The European Union is galvanising such formidable bloc that it may even subsequently marginalize the United Nations. Western countries are now seeing boundaries as bridges, not barriers. Their national sovereignties are beginning to dovetail with each other to the point where regional citizenship is gaining precedence over national identities. It becomes clear that Africa must adapt or die to this changing time and clime.

Africa has spent close to four decades networking with international organisations, which have little or no respect for the African personality. As Africans we have been so infatuated with international solidarity that we have abandoned our interests in favour of neo-colonial associations like the Commonwealth, Francophonie etc. It is time to re-examine these neo-colonial umbilical cords. This is the moment to erect a union that is pro-African in terms of economic parity and political integrity. The new challenges Africa faces today require a viable supra-national structure, which on the 9th of July 2002 was, called the African Union. As I see it, this structure can be perfected along one of these two strategies (a) the African five regions or (A-5) strategy (b) the European Union or (E. U.) strategy.

The African Union: A-5 Strategy

Africa can be mapped into five sub-regions, North, South, East, West and Central (forget about the neo-colonial nomenclature of Francophone Africa, Anglophone Africa, Lusophone Africa etc. and remember we are Bantuphone Africa). Each sub-region is equipped with viable economic blocs. These blocs, which serve to maintain regional security and economic co-operation include, the Maghreb Union in the North; Southern African Development community (SADC) in the South; East African Co-operation (EAC) in the East; Economic Community for West African States (ECOWAS) in the West; and the Central African Economic and Monetary Union (CEMAC) in the Central sub-region. Though other micro blocs do exist (some acting as neo-colonial saboteurs) within Africa, the five mentioned above have over the years proven their mettle in structural and institutional designs, albeit with varying success. By setting up these communities, politicians and economic planners hoped to overcome more quickly the causes of underdevelopment, to help create a basis for resolving conflicts between neighbouring countries and to reduce the commercial, industrial, technical and financial dependency of most Third World countries on the industrial nation in the north (Zehender, 1988: 51).

The aim of regional blocs has always revolved around a shared interest among geographical neighbours and an eventual common dream among the African people. Indeed, Nkrumah's dream with the Casablanca group was shattered because the Monrovia group believed in a gradual integration of African countries through regional co-operation. Unfortunately, all attempts to foster a smooth regional co-operation have resulted instead in regional destabilisation in some cases and outright nonchalance in most cases. Pragmatic economic agendas like the Lagos Plan of Action (1980) and the African Economic Community Treaty of Abuja (1991) proposed by economic planners and signed by heads of states have remained mere pipe dreams and pan African demagogy. The result is that today, the legitimate aspirations of genuine African unity as conceived by the people continues to be at the periphery of the agenda of ego-bloated African leaders.

Many reasons have already been advanced by other scholars for the failure of rapid economic integration that could have led to a United Africa. Among these reasons, one must single out the lack of political will by our leaders to first of all provide structural stability through good governance within their own countries and then to relinquish their colonial sovereignties and the "sacrosanctity of boundaries" to the common cause of African unity.

Reluctant to chart its own path to economic development, Africa has turned International Monetary Fund (I.M.F.) loans into neo-colonial blessings and political victories. Yet, no one can honestly deny that the worst economic performance has been during the era of structural adjustment. This is because instead of pursuing the goal of diversifying and transforming the economy, "African countries have been forced to embark on a structural adjustment paradigm whose objective is to perpetuate its mono cultural economic system, its narrow production base and the persistence of a high level of external dependence which renders it highly susceptible to external shocks" (Adedeji, 1997: 9). Again, African scholars have provided alternative frameworks to structural adjustment for socio-economic recovery and transformation, which no leader has taken seriously. "The West is always insisting on continuous lowering of prices of Africa's raw materials and on the regular devaluation of Africa's currencies. In order to pay for its imports and to service its debts, Africa is forced to sell more of its raw materials. How can Africa achieve any economic growth under such neo colonialist exploitation?" (Chimutengvende, 1997: 15). And so because each time the European economy sneezes, the African economy catches a cold, Africa alone is home to 32 of the 47 "poorest" countries in the world.

Until Africans challenge the dangerously utopian pretensions of the I.M.F. and opt for a union that emphasises a sustainable, human-centred, holistic development paradigm, we shall remain at the bottom of the economic pyramid. One can only hope that African leaders have now read the handwriting on the wall and that they could commit the A-5 strategy, thus building the five sub-regional organisations until the continent becomes a five-tiered federation with a political executive organ at the top. Africa would then be comprised of five large interdependent federations instead of fifty-three autonomous but weak nation states. The next step would be for these sub-regional federations to address security and economic issues, adopt a single sub-regional African language, create a common sub-regional passport, introduce a single sub-regional currency and establish a single sub-regional parliament. The results would be that Africa would have five main African languages, five main passports, five main currencies and five main parliaments. The federated sub-regions would develop adequate transport and communication infrastructure, share in food security and allow for free movement of goods and people within them.

At the continental level, there would be a political executive organ that would co-ordinate all the activities of the five sub-regions. This is the organ that would be truly the African Union.

The African Union would have a supranational secretariat, and representatives from the sub-regions would constitute the federal executive body of the Union. To promote collegial leadership, the representation from the sub-regions shall be heads of states who may have been elected to co-ordinate the activities of their sub-regions.

Therefore, there would be five heads of state to run the executive arm of the Union at every given time.

Clearly, the A-5 strategy calls for a radical change of mentality among our leaders. If the present state of activities inherent in the three already active sub-regional organizations (ECOWAS, EAC, SADC) can be a basis upon which to judge, the verdict would be that there is reason to believe in a vibrant and enterprising five-tiered federation of Africa. However, for an African Union built on the A-5 strategy to survive, the federated sub-regions must overcome cultural imperialistic prejudices, personality rivalries, hegemonistic tendencies, national chauvinism and unbridled power interest. But, as Diop has argued, "The time has come for us to abandon our complexes and work in favour of a Union that is favourable to all Africans. That's the crux of the matter" (1987: 112).

The African Union - The E.U Strategy

The present African Union structure seems to have been fashioned along the lines of the European Union, but not along the dreams of the Sirte Declaration of 9 September 1999. To blend these two components the African Union members should continue to ponder over these objectives:

- To institute a new African nationalism of self-confidence and Unity among the people of Africa.
- To eradicate all vestiges of colonialism and neo-colonialism in Africa.
- To promote indigenous democracy, endogenous development and sustainable peace.
- To safeguard the common values, fundamental interests and independence of the Union.
- To strengthen issues of co-operations, stability and development of the Union and its member states in all ways.

- To review areas of debts, trade and co-operation with Western countries.

These objectives should provide the union with a vision for a shared future - providing for all its members balanced development, political stability and economic independence. In order to achieve these objectives, the Union should uphold the following principles:
- Member states shall renounce a definite portion of their national sovereignty to independent institutions and the general Union.
- Member states shall adopt a single flag, a single anthem, a single passport, a single African currency, and a single African language.
- There shall be no discrimination based on nationality against any citizen seeking employment outside their own member states; in other words each citizen shall move, work and reside anywhere within the member states.
- There shall be harmonised rules and access to public sector jobs and benefits derived therefrom; with priority given to citizens from member states.
- There shall be a review of the educational system, so it serves the needs of the majority of Africans and a harmonised recognition of diplomas and certificates.
- There shall be abolition of customs or tax barriers and limited border checks so as to ensure the free movement of persons and goods across boundaries and to establish a common market and economic community.
- Members shall be absolutely dedicated to the economic, cultural and political unification of Africa.
- Members shall share a common ideological platform on foreign, security and agricultural policies.
- No other international co-operation by member states shall be done to undermine the charter of the Union.

The Question of Language and Education

One phenomenon that would have to be stressed in both the A-5 and E-U strategies is the need for a single language and currency for member states. When we know that our thought process and development priorities are influenced by language, we can estimate how much harm the continuous presence of colonial languages have had on our mental, cultural, economic and historical spheres of life. It is time we selected a continental language, one that will be taught formally in schools especially as our school curricula are full of irrelevant and cultural deviant subjects.

What is the relevance of Latin, German and Spanish to a Cameroonian child who already has to grapple with his mother's tongue (National Language), and to learn English and French in a so-called official bilingual nation? Why should the Nigerian or Equator-Guinean child be bamboozled with the French Language after he has acquired his national languages and learnt English and Spanish respectively? By the time the child graduates from school, he is able to communicate outside the continent, yet incapable of communicating with his fellow Africans. This tower of Babel must be destroyed. Many foreign embassies in Africa have set up language learning facilities to non-native speakers. After choosing the single African language, African embassies shall institute linguistic centres for the teaching of this language. Member states of the Union shall adopt one foreign language (of their choice) and a single African language as official languages. Policies should be established so as to propagate the teaching and learning of the African language through formal and informal sections and from the nursery to adult schools. The controversy over which language to choose amongst the 2034 languages in Africa is a non-event, a mere escapism to delay a genuine idea and an intellectual gimmick for emasculated linguists in Africa. If we chose foreign languages because of colonial contacts, how come we are still learning languages of other foreign countries with which we had no historical alliance? If the reasons are not mere individual elevations of social status or piggish economic courtship then it is outright manifestation of our habitual pinheaded policies. And the foreign linguistic invasion of Africa is far from being over - even the Chinese, Japanese, and Russians are brandishing their technology in exchange for cultural assimilation. Without a language whose roots come from African soil, 80% of the population shall be excluded in development policies. It is a considered view that Africans will make their own contribution to science and technology only when original African thoughts, ideas and methods of production based on African culture and rooted in its own ecology can emerge (Afolayan, 1982: 186). Indeed, the issue of a continental language has such far-reaching consequence for the present and future developments of Africa that it deserves the same urgent and serious attention as economic and political unification of Africa. At this juncture I still make bold to propose Swahili as the official language for all Africans. The 2004 African Union summit used Swahili as a working language. Individual countries can carry out other policies affecting their own national languages.

Tied to our obnoxious language policy is the obsolete educational system that has served the interest of the elite to the detriment of the masses. It is no secret that our present colonial education has produced a kind of colonial intelligentsia who have become the very architects of colonial enslavement. Education should empower the individual to take or make decisions about his own life. The purpose of proper education is not to drive the individual towards a symbol status or material arrogance but to prepare him to be a responsible handler of power. Unfortunately, in spite of decades of erudition in science and Arts, Africans are still copycats instead of manufacturers; repairers instead of inventors. We have become receptacles of transferred knowledge instead of moulders of indigenous knowledge thus giving rise to a generation of geniuses in colonial education but cretins in African education. The crisis in African education is really a crisis in African self-confidence. Even the little inventions that have been conceived by our own folks are repudiated and recklessly snubbed by Africans themselves in favour of what is banally called "original" i.e. made in France, Britain or Germany.

African governments have stifled local initiatives by cut-throat taxes or simply allowed the inundation of our market with foreign goods for individual kickbacks. Our new path to self-help and self-reliant community education should not sever us from the universal values of scholarship; yet we must refocus towards an education that offers vocational opportunities and creates self-employment. We need an education that emphasises production and manufacturing; an education that tells our real history and the potentials inherent in home grown development; an education which makes Africans see themselves through their own eyes; an education that seeks to restore the dignity of the African civilisation and to reinforce the concept of African indigenous common market. We must go on asking this age-old question "Education for what purpose?" There is a need now for a generation of Africans to be educated in Africa by other Africans for the express purpose of serving Africa. To break away from mental slavery, we must reclaim the minds of our young people-those minds that have been cloistered by the colonial phantasms of supremacy and the hypnotic opium of superhighway technology (what is an Internet without a Roadnet?) There has been a false propaganda that Africa is running a development race with the West. How absurd! When this same West has retarded the development of Africa by slavery, colonialism and imperialism: Africa is running a race with itself, and from the examples of Nagasaki and Hiroshima, it shall build its own future. We must teach our children at home, in the streets, everywhere, the kind of education that transforms our own raw materials to the kind of finished product we need. And this kind of education can be instituted in pan African community centres whose curricula should emphasise subjects of skilled labour relevant to our employment and private sector market, and also in our tertiary level where African Studies and subjects of appropriate sciences and technology are shamelessly absent.

The Question of Currency

As for the question of an African currency, it is indeed abashing that our economic tails are still tied to the apron strings of the IMF and World Bank. So every time the Bretton Woods decide to depreciate our economic independence they devalue their money. Countries in CFA zone have been made to believe that only the French franc can save them from their corruption syndrome. It is even more ludicrous for someone who has travelled within the continent to realise how national currencies are rejected for US dollars, French franc and English sterling pound. Europe has had the vision, courage and political will to introduce a single currency. Europe has a right to its financial independence but so does Africa. The creation of a single currency will be the greatest structural change that will be a blessing to Africans all over the world. The new currency for Africa will be backed by a common market and an enormous Gross national product (G. N. P), its value will increase tremendously. This will make the single currency for Africa competitive in international transactions. Africa's resources and its ability to convert these resources (natural and human) to their fullest potential through a common market will make Africa's single currency one of the strongest in the world. That single currency should be called AMU (African Monetary Unit) (Nvenge, 1989:26-27). Another pan Africanist, Maurice Tadadjeu proposes the creation of a common currency especially among sub-regional groups. This common currency could either be the cowrie (reference to precolonial currency of Africa) or another currency which he calls AFRI (root word for AFRICA) (Tadadjeu, 1996: 107). There can be no effective common market or African Economic community without a single currency among the member states of the African Union. A single currency will be the beginning of an economic Assertion; a break with the dependency and domination syndrome that has made the continent extremely powerless in the face of Global Competition. A single African currency must replace weak national currencies and must give the average African a sense of continental belonging. This will also require either fortifying the structures of the African Development Bank or setting up an African investment Bank. It took the European Union three stages with a life span of seven years to realise the dream of a single currency. But above all it took a political will and the pressure of the citizens to turn that dream into a reality. Africa can also perform its own miracles.

The African Union shall accomplish its set objectives and principles through including or strengthening the following main institutions: -
(i)   African Parliament (The Great Indaba)
(ii)   Council of State
(iii) Peace and Security Council
(iv)   Pan African Media Council
(v)   Development/Solidarity Fund
(vi)   Court of Auditors

(i)   The African Parliament shall be the supreme institution of the Union. It shall in the true African tradition be the main decision-making body (The Great Indaba) with decisions arrived at by consensus or by a qualified majority vote. It shall draw its members by continental universal suffrage. Members must have a supranational, democratic and foresighted vision. They shall have a five-year mandate renewable once. The parliament shall have both executive and legislative powers in the Union. Its decisions shall be binding to all member state. It shall set up its internal general secretariat.

(ii)   The Council of state shall be a nucleus of those with ministerial portfolios from member states. These ministers could be called Ministers of African Affairs. The council of state shall have specialised technical committees in the Union. These committees shall reflect the terms of reference of national cabinets. The members of these specialised committees shall prepare projects and programs and submit them to the parliament for debate. The members shall seek to harmonise and co-ordinate national policies to reflect the purposes of the Union. They shall be expected to carry out, in their respective countries, decision from the parliament. While they act as the mouthpieces of their respective governments and people, within the Union, they work together in the fraternal spirit of continental unity and in the pragmatic vision of people-centred Union. Operating in a supranational manner the council remains responsible to the African parliament.

(iii) The Peace and Security Council shall consist of eminent state persons in Africa. These state persons shall be respected former Heads of States, traditional rulers, scholars, activists etc. - people who have proven and continue to prove their dedication to the welfare of the African people. This council shall be an autonomous body with a Peace Fund. Contributions towards this Peace Fund shall come from a percentage of member states' national police force budget and donations from friends of Africa. The council shall in support with local non-governmental organisations (N.G.O), the media, traditional rulers, and other traditional bases for conflict prevention set up an early warning signal in member states. It shall monitor talks on constitutional reforms, electoral processes, assist in referendums and institute a campaign on civic education (the value of indigenous democracy and development) and a culture of peace. It shall propose sanctions to the African parliament on members that violate basic democratic and human right principles. It shall re-establish "Try African-security council first" approach with other international organisations to avoid cultural embarrassments, ideological double standards and bureaucratic red tapes. As for the creation of a Pan-African peacekeeping police force, the council shall either keep a permanent force drawn from the peace keeping police forces from member states or appoint a National Force to keep peace in another member state. The primordial role of the Council shall be to exhaust all avenues of conflict prevention through the traditional wisdom of dialogue and concertation. This way hopefully structural conflict shall be prevented from escalating to armed conflicts.

(iv) The Pan African Media Council shall be charged with monitoring Africa's image in the media. Apart from countering the selective distorted image portrayed by the European-created media, this organ shall gather, produce and disseminate material relevant to the history, cultural values, and development-priorities of the African continent. According to Clarke, the mass media, aimed at oppressed people in particular and African people in general, is part of an attempt at controlling the minds of the world (Clarke, 1992: 338). Our youths grow up seeing themselves through Western binoculars; they inculcate obscene, individualistic and material values produced on our electronic and print media; they see alien role models as the only way to cheap heroism.

It is the Western media that nourish Africa's youth with a bizarre life style, misplaced priorities, and a gargantuan capitalist appetite. Our society has been infested with the abscess of want and waste to the extent that the traditional ethic of frugality and sharing is dying. The Western media have had the greatest control on the minds of the African youth in particular to the extent that mental and cultural imperialism will remain the greatest battle to be fought in the years ahead. Maybe the creation of an African youth forum will be the beginning of a solution. We need a press that serves the interest of the ordinary African, not the ego of African Heads of State. We need a press that propagates Unity and Co-operation in Africa, not a sectarian and xenophobic hate press. We must be in control of our own media; World news that is defined by the West excludes and distorts non-western values. We need therefore to "look deep into ourselves and what the propaganda of the Western media has done to us and how we have played a role in spreading this propaganda. Anybody who accepts all the propaganda they see about black men and black women proves that they don't understand the dispensers of the propaganda and they don't understand black men and black women or themselves. I believe that once we change the image of ourselves, we will change the image of humanity, and subsequently we will change the power structure of the whole world and leave for generations still unborn a map and a plan of courage in nation-building that will last and change the world. We are perhaps the only people that can do this because, since we gave the world the first humanity, we can give the world a new humanity at a time when it needs it most (Clarke, 1992: 362-363). The pan African media council shall therefore institute an authoritative African news Agency that shall condition our entry into a new world information order on our ability to winnow or filter the kind of information and images that other people conjure for us. We should expose our people to positive and developmental journalism so they plough their future not on the shifting sands of war, poverty and disease but on the solid rock of development and good governance. Finally, if we must realise the dream of reinforcing Pan African News Agency (PANA) and ``Union des Radio et Televisions Nationales de l'Afrique'' (URTNA) or setting up an authentic, indigenous and authoritative African news Agency, then we must invest heavily in the communication industry. We have paid lip service to this sector of our national life and others have exploited it. Since "what we do for ourselves depends on what we are willing to accept about ourselves and what we know of ourselves", we must make investment in the communication industry a priority.

(v) A Development and solidarity Fund shall be set up in the African Union. This Fund is different from other specialised funds of the institutions of the Union - it operates on the principle that Africa shall develop on self-reliance and solidarity. It shall be a communal bank for member states with money accruing from:

(a) Annual contributions from member states (this annual contribution shall be derived from a designed percentage of each member's national budget and the sum shall be paid at a specific month of the year).

(b) Unconditional donations from friends of Africa; such friends could be International organisations, personalities, non governmental organisations etc.

(c) Domestic savings from member states provided they agree that the amount shall be published in their respective states annually,

(d) Special development and solidarity contract with Africans in the Diaspora.

It is by sheer accident that some Africans away from home are called Jamaicans, Trinidadians, Barbadians, African Americans etc. They are all African people

92

reacting to different forms of oppression (Clarke, 1992,: 419). The era of wearing a betraying sense of anger or false spirit of superiority is gone. Together we are in the same boat, we either swim or sink. The days of emotive intellectual discourses on slavery are over; the concept of nostalgic homecoming meetings with African tin-gods should be re-examined; the days of touristic sojourns to the land of our ancestors are ticking away; in front of us lie the days of building concrete bridges to Africa. We must connect with each other "The Jews in America proudly relate and do business with Israel. Italian Americans are well connected with their people in Italy. The Chinese and Japanese Americans have a direct relationship with their people overseas. Again only people who historically have been deliberately miseducated and brainwashed through negative press and cannot connect and relate fully with the land of their ancestors are the Africans in America" (Nvenge, 1989 : 33). Our brothers and sisters who by history or choice are under foreign skies, should help repair the damage caused by four centuries of slavery, one century of colonialism and half a century of prebendal politics in Africa. Only money (in cash or in kind) can do the trick not tears nor talks. Plough your hard currency or development expertise into the development and solidarity fund and ask for a receipt. That receipt is your symbolic commitment to the survival and prosperity of our people.

Money from the development and solidarity fund shall be used: -

- to help member states in natural and man-made disasters,
- to assist member states in specific development projects endorsed by the Union
- to loan to member states (an alternative to SAP/IMF loan) with well-defined projects (money paid back at a precise period and on a soft interest).

In all cases, beneficiaries shall be those contributing regularly and those who accept that a commission follows up the execution of the projects.

(vi) Court of Auditors:
The court of Auditors is the tax payers "representative, responsible for checking that the African Union spends its money according to its budgetary rules and regulation and for the purposes for which it is intended". It shall, like the European Court of Auditors, be an independent institution, which scrutinises moral, administrative and accounting principles of all the other institutions and makes its report to the African parliament. It shall also serve as a preventive mechanism by identifying errors, investigating irregularities and potential cases of fraud and making them known to the relevant institution for action to be taken. For their part, if the institutions feel they need guidance on some aspects of their management of funds, they can ask the court for an opinion and must do so before adopting documents relating to financial regulation and own resources. It is worthy of note that all the institutions of the African Union shall work closely together in constructive co-operation for the benefit of the people of Africa.

I want to conclude this chapter on the note that whatever strategy we choose A5 or EU, African unity already prevails in the grassroots. All we need now is the formalisation of certain symbols and institutions to allow for the free interaction of people and goods. Most of the hair saloon business in Cameroon are owned by Ghanaians; the few African owned-shops in Zimbabwe are controlled by Nigerians; we could expand further by allowing Cameroonian restaurant owners to operate in the South African region; Senegalese dressmakers to operate in the East African region; South African jewellers in Central Africa, East African teachers in North Africa and North

African shoemakers in West Africa. Agricultural expertise in Botswana and Cape Verde could be exported to other countries of the African Union. The policy of trade by barter between member states should be revived. We reject Western multinational hegemony and Greek, Lebanese and Asian petty trade monopoly. With a reasonable continental policy based on intra African trade and co-operation through the African Union, Africans shall work for the prime benefit of Africa. The ruling elites and the enthusiastic masses shall together embark on a journey in which we all see Africa not as a conglomeration of nations with artificial and psychological boundaries but as a political Union that seeks a better quality of life, through participatory governance, integrated and self-reliant economics and more integrity for the African people.

AFTERWORD

Way Forward for Africa, by George Ngwane engages the reader in a candid and committed discussion of the challenges of participatory democracy and leadership for the African youth within the backdrop of contending ideological values like globalization, Pan-Africanism, and African renaissance.

The author's insight into the role of the youths in African traditional governance, the contending models of democratisation in the continent, and the process of interest aggregation within party, non-party and civil society structures, as well as his ability to weave in a coherent manner the burning issues of generational politics and governance into the strategic vision of the new people-centered African Union are quite educative.

The author equally appeals to the mostly complacent African youths of the "wasted independence generation" to emulate great world and African leaders of past generations by taking their responsibilities within the current processes of democratic transition and nation-building. In this way, he breaks away from most analysts of conventional wisdom, who blame inadequate youth participation in the continent's political governance solely on their exclusion by the older generations.

Ngwane's appeal is equally challenging because it comes at a time when hypocrisy, clientilism, opportunism, poor mentoring, youth unemployment, and a reverse brain drain of educated African youths into Western countries as political and economic asylum-seekers have all contributed to poor youth governance, and their ability to take the type of responsibilities he imagines are required of them.

Youth governance in Africa has remained high in the strategic vision of most international and regional organisations because the youths make up 60-70% of the populations of African countries. Moreover, it is these African youths who as leaders by 2015 will be called to implement the UN Millennium Development Goals (MDGs), and other long-term strategic plans and visions developed at international, continental, and national levels in the continent.

The issue of youth governance in Africa, which includes youth unemployment, youth leadership, youth participation in political governance, the changing role of the African universities, and the role of youths in promoting peace and security in the continent, has therefore been the focus of a number of international and regional initiatives.

Some of such international initiatives have included the conferences by the African Leadership Forum in Abuja (April 1999), the Pan-African Youth Movement (2000), the OAU (2001), and the ECA symposium on youth governance (October 2004). Another initiative on the subject worth mentioning is CODESRIA's special programme on youth governance, which has been promoting dialogue on the issue. More importantly, youth leadership and governance in Africa will be the theme of the fifth African Development Forum (ADF V), to be organised by the ECA and other stakeholders around 2006.

Way Forward for Africa is therefore not only topical, but also provides a useful contribution to the on-going debate on generational politics, which is not unique to Africa, and which because of its growing international attention, most African countries will be bound to submit their best practices and country profiles on the issue.

Definitely, the book is not an exhaustive discussion of the topic, and some of the author's conclusions are still debatable. However, his courage and attempt to promote public education and debate on the burning issue of youth governance only reinforces his image and role as a true "African Mwalimu", committed to a vocation which makes the general public an amphitheatre, and a marketplace of ideas.

It is for this reason that I find Ngwane's book timely, educative, and a useful contribution to the on-going debate on generational politics and youth governance in Africa. I will therefore recommend the book to readers of African politics, history, anthropology, and the sociology of power.

Churchill Ewumbue-Monono
Minister Plenipotentiary

BIBLIOGRAPHY

Adedeji, Adebayo (1997). "What prospects for Nigerian political economy in the next millennium?" *in African Today*, vol. 3, No. 4.

Arifalo, S. O. (1982). "The military in contemporary African politics" in *African History and Culture*, Nigeria: Longman.

Ashunkem, N. (1996). "International Economic advantages of an African Union", unpublished paper.

Ayittey, George B. N. (1992). *Africa Betrayed*, New York: St. Martin's Press.

Bejuka, G. (1996). "The urgent need for an Economic Integration in Africa" unpublished paper.

Bratton, M. (1993). "Political Liberalization in Africa in the 1990s: advances and set backs" in *Economic Reform in Africa's New Era of Political Liberalization*, Washington: Workshop paper.

Burgsdorff, Sven. (1992). "Consociational Democracy: A New Concept for Africa" in *The Courier*, no. 134.

Chafe, K. S. (1994). "The problematic of African Democracy in Nigeria" in *AFRIKA ZAMANI*, No 2, CODESRIA publications.

Chege, Michael. (1995). "The military in the Transition to Democracy in Africa" in *CODESRIA Bulletin*, No. 3.

Chimutengwende, C. (1997). "Pan Africanism and the second liberation of Africa" in *CODESRIA Bulletin*, No. 2.

Clarke, John H. (1992). *Africans at the crossroads*, New Jersey: African World Press, Inc.

Davidson, Basil. (1992). *The Black Man's Burden*, New York : Times Books.

Diop, Cheikh Anta. (1987). *Black Africa: The Economic and Cultural Basis for a Federated State,* New Jersey: Africa World Press/Lawrence Hill.

Ebini, Christmas A. (1997). "We present peace and Appeal to the Heavenly Council" in *The Cryer*, Vol. 1, No. 5.

European Union. (1996). *Serving the European Union,* Luxemburg.

Global Coalition for Africa, (1992). *Documents on: development, democracy and debt.* The Hague.

Joseph, Richard. ed. (1978). *Gaullist Africa: Cameroon under Ahmadou Ahidjo,* Enugu: Fourth Dimension Publishers.

Mazrui, Ali. (1986). *The Africans.* London: BBC Publications.

_ _ _. (1992)."Elements of the New Africa" in *Index on Censorship*, No. 4.

Mbuyinga, Eyenga. (1982). *Pan Africanism or Neocolonialism, the Bankruptcy of the O. A. U.,* London : Zed Press.

Moroney, Eliteed. (1989).*AFRICA* vol. 1, New York : Facts on File Publications.

Moshoeshoe, II. (1992). "Give us back our democracy". in Index on censorship, No 4.

Mwohora, E. (1994). "La democratrisation au Burundi: heritages et conflit ethniques, 1959-1993, in *AFRIKA ZAMANI*, No. 2, CODESRIA publications.

Ngwane, George. (2000). "Settling Disputes in Africa", Denver: International Academic Publishers.

_ _ _. (1996). "Burundi's burden and Buyoya's blueprint", unpublished paper.

_ _ _. (1996). "Establishing an African Security Council" unpublished paper.

_ _ _. (1996). "Abuja's Treaty, Africa's Economic Miracle" in *Africa Star International*, Vol. 1, No. 1.

Nnoli, Okwudiba. (1995). *Ethnic conflicts and Democratisation in Africa,* Dakar : CODESRIA paper.

Nvenge, A. P. K. (1995). *African Unity - The only solution,* Brooklyn: African Unity Press.

Olaniyam, Richard. ed. (1982). *African History and Culture,* Nigeria: Longman.

Prah, Kwesi. (1997). *Accusing the victims - In my father's house,* in CODESRIA bulletin, No 1.

Rodney, Walter. (1972). *How Europe underdeveloped Africa,* London: Bogle-L'Ouverture publications.

Samantha, Anderson, trans. (1988). *Thomas Sankara speaks: The Burkina Faso Revolution, 1983-1987,* New York : Pathfinder Press.

Soyinka, Wole (1996). *The Open Sore of a Continent,* USA : Oxford University Press.

Tadadjeu, Maurice (1996). Confederation des Etats - Unis d'Afrique, Yaounde: Buma Kor Publishers.

Tande, Dibussi: (1995). "Political Pluralism and Authoritarian Continuity", in *The Journal of National Union of Cameroonian students, Great Britain and Northern Ireland,* Vol. 7.

Zehender, W. (1988). "Regional Cooperation in perspective - some experiences in sub-Saharan Africa" in *The Courier,* no. 121.

Zeleza, Paul T. (1994). "Reflections on the Traditions of Authoritarianism and Democracy in African History" in *AFRIKA ZAMANI,* No. 2, CODESRIA publications.

NOTES

Africa Forum, a private quarterly magazine published in New York.

Africa Star, a private magazine published in Limbe, Cameroon.

Africa Today, a private quarterly magazine published in London.

Basic Texts of the Cameroon National Union (C.N.U), a political manifesto of the former and lone party in Cameroon.

Basic Texts of Cameroon People's Democratic Movement (C P D M) - a political manifesto of a party in Cameroon.

CNU Constitution, a party document.

CNU Militants Guide, a party document.

CODESRIA bulletin, a quarterly bulletin meant for African social science research published by the Council for the Development of Social Science in Africa, Dakar Senegal.

The Courier, published every two months by the commission of European communities, Brussels.

The Cryer, a monthly magazine for the African community published in the United States, and dedicated to the promotion of Pan Africanism.

Index on Censorship, a privately-owned bimonthly published in London, by Writers and Scholars International Ltd.

Tam-tam, a publication by the Information and Communications Desk of the All Africa Conference of Churches, Nairobi - Kenya.

West Africa, a privately-owned weekly, London.

INDEX

Democracy
Chipenda, Jose, 31
Chirac, Jacques, 23
Choice, Conservative, 25; Innovative 25,30
Christianity, 4,5,6,17
Civilization 15,17
Colonialism, 3,5,17,19,20,69
Commonwealth, 5,6,5
Comoros, 5
Complacent Generation, 1-3
Conferences, transition 19,20,22,24
                    sovereign national, 25
Council of Elders, 16,18
Critical generation, 8-13

D
Davidson, Basil, 19,44,57
Debate, 14
Decentralisation, 26,*see also* democracy
Democracy,   14,15,   Precolonial   Democracy,15-16,19,20
Multiparty,   25,26,27,28;   Umbrella,32;   No   party,   38;
Consociational 45; Monarchal 49
Dependency, 5
Diaspora,78
Dibussi, Tande, 11
Diop Anta Cheikh,65,68,69
Dubois, W.E.B, 7

E
East African Community, 65,68
Ebini, Atem, 6
ECOWAS, 65,68
Education, 11
Elders, *see* Council of Elders
Elections, 15,22,23, *see also* democracy
Elites, 19,20,21, *see also* leadership
Empires, 16
Europe, Supremacy of, 5
European Union, 65,69,79

L

Lagos Plan of Action, 66
Language (African), 66,67,71-72, *see also*
Kiswahili; Foreign, 74,72
Leaders/Leadership, African, 13,14,15,19
Lesotho, 54
Letsie, David King, 54
Lumumba, Patrice, 13

M

Maghreb Union, 64
Manifesto, 22,23,26
Market (common), 68,69,70
Masire, Quett, 13
Mazrui, Ali, 18,31,35,58,60
Mboya, Tom, 31
Mbuza, 25
Media Council (Pan-African), 76,77
Media, 27
Military, 58; *see also* Army
Mobutu, 13,60
Mohammed, Murtala, 60
Monarchical Democracy, 49
Monrovia Group, 66
Moroney, Sean, 54
Moshoeshoe, King, 24
Mswati, King, 51
Multiparty Democracy, 25,26,27,28
Museveni, Yoweri, 13,39,41-42
Mworoha, E, 218

N

National Conference, *see* Conferences
Ndaba, 29,84
Neocolonalism, *see* Colonisation
Nigeria, 37, 38, 39
Nkrumah, Kwame, 10,14
Nnoli Okwudiba, 22,30,35

Non Governmental Organisations, 85
No-Party Democracy, 44
Nvenge Amentu, 83,88
Nyerere Julius, 14,22,35,40

O
Obasanjo, Olesugun, 12
Obote, Milton, 31
Ogbonna, Nicholas, 48
Organisation of African Unity (O..A.U), 9,24
        Charter,20; Problems, 64
Oyowe, 55

P
Palaver Theory, 16
Pan Africanism, 7,8; Kinds, 8-10
PANA, 77
Pantheon, 4
Parliament (African), 67,75
Parties, Political, 14; One Party System, 20;
                Local Names, 22
                Multiparty, 23 - 24
Passport (African),67,70
Peterson, Hector, 11
Police Force, 62-63,75
Political System, 25, *see also* Choice
Power, 12,18; Transfer of, 19, 19, 30
Prah, Kwesi, 3,
Prayers, 5
Precolonial Democracy, 15-16, 18,19
Press, 75,76-71
Protests, Sharpeville, 3, 11
South Africa, 11
                Soweto, 11

R
Rawlings, Jerry, 11
Rebellion, *see* Protests
Referendum, 25

Renaissance, (African) 2,9,12
Revolution, 43-44
Rice, Susan, 42
Rodney, Walter, 16,17,18
Rwanda, 56

S
Salim, Salim, Ahmed, 32
Samantha, 39
Sankara, Thomas, 36, 39-42
SAP, 67,79
Security Council (African),75,76
Senghor, Leopold, 13
Slavery, 6, 7,9
Sobhuza, King, 51
Southern African Development Community (SADC), 65,68
Sovietisation, 8
Soyinka, Wole, 59
State Authority, 26-28
State Paralysis,28-30
Sullivan, Leon, 7
Supranationalism, 27
Swaziland, 50,51
Sycophants, 8,7,27

T
Tadadjeu, Maurice, 74
Tanzania, 35,38
Tinkhundla, 51
Toure, Sekou, 13
Toure, Toumani Amadou, 61
Trade, 65,66,79-80
Tutsis, 18,55

U
URTNA, 77
Umbrella Democracy, 32
Uganda, 31-32,39,41-42
Union, Students, 9,11, AFRICAN, 66-71

Ujamaa, 16,19

V
Village, Assembly, 16
Voice of America (VOA), 42

W
Wasted Generation, 3-7
West African Students' Union (WASU), 11
Western, Civilisation, 5; Media,5,76
            Standards, 3; Models, 4,5
Whiteman, 4, 5
World Bank, 22,30,73
World News, 76

X
Xenophobia, 76,77

Y
Youths (African), 1, 9

Z
Zehender, 66
Zimbabwe, 89